Understanding the
Fundamentals of Music
Part I

Professor Robert Greenberg

THE TEACHING COMPANY ®

PUBLISHED BY:

THE TEACHING COMPANY
4151 Lafayette Center Drive, Suite 100
Chantilly, Virginia 20151-1232
1-800-TEACH-12
Fax—703-378-3819
www.teach12.com

ISBN 1-59803-287-9

Robert Greenberg, Ph.D.

San Francisco Performances

Robert Greenberg was born in Brooklyn, New York, in 1954 and has lived in the San Francisco Bay area since 1978. He received a B.A. in music, magna cum laude, from Princeton University in 1976, where his principal teachers were Edward Cone, Daniel Werts, and Carlton Gamer in composition; Claudio Spies and Paul Lansky in analysis; and Jerry Kuderna in piano. In 1984, he received a Ph.D. in music composition, with distinction, from the University of California, Berkeley, where his principal teachers were Andrew Imbrie and Olly Wilson in composition and Richard Felciano in analysis.

Professor Greenberg has composed more than 45 works for a wide variety of instrumental and vocal ensembles. His works have been performed in New York, San Francisco, Chicago, Los Angeles, England, Ireland, Greece, Italy, and the Netherlands, where the Amsterdam Concertgebouw performed his *Child's Play* for String Quartet. His numerous honors include three Nicola de Lorenzo Composition Prizes and three Meet-the-Composer Grants. Recent commissions have come from the Koussevitzky Foundation at the Library of Congress, the Alexander String Quartet, the San Francisco Contemporary Music Players, San Francisco Performances, the Strata Ensemble, and the XTET ensemble.

Professor Greenberg is a board member and an artistic director of COMPOSERS, INC., a composers' collective/production organization based in San Francisco. His music is published by Fallen Leaf Press and CPP/Belwin and is recorded on the Innova label. He has performed, taught, and lectured extensively across North America and Europe. He is currently music-historian-in-residence with San Francisco Performances, where he has lectured and performed since 1994, and resident composer and music historian to National Public Radio's "Weekend All Things Considered." He has served on the faculties of the University of California at Berkeley, California State University at Hayward, and the San Francisco Conservatory of Music, where he chaired the Department of Music, History and Literature from 1989–2001 and served as the Director of the Adult Extension Division from 1991–1996.

Professor Greenberg has lectured for some of the most prestigious musical and arts organizations in the United States, including the San Francisco Symphony (where, for 10 years, he was host and lecturer for the symphony's nationally acclaimed "Discovery Series"), the Lincoln Center for the Performing Arts, the Van Cliburn Foundation, and the Chautauqua Institute. He is a sought-after lecturer for businesses and business schools, speaking at such diverse organizations as the Commonwealth Club of San Francisco and the University of Chicago Graduate School of Business, and has been profiled in various major publications, including the *Wall Street Journal*, *Inc.* magazine, and the London *Times*.

Table of Contents
Understanding the Fundamentals of Music
Part I

Understanding the Fundamentals of Music

Scope:

Understanding how music is created is comparable to understanding how a language is constructed. Like a language, music has a syntax, a vocabulary. We start by listening to that language. We first learn to distinguish different sonic and temporal phenomena; then, we come to understand how those phenomena are interrelated. After that, we can begin to understand how and why we perceive structural integrity and expressive meaning in a given section of music.

Given the constraints of a course such as this, we will not learn how to read and write music. This course, then, is about using our ears, about discovering and exploring musical syntax through our ears by learning what the parts of the musical language *sound* like, rather than what they *look* like on paper. This is an infinitely more useful skill than simply learning to recognize musical constructs on paper with our eyes because we can apply such listening skills to almost any piece of music in almost any style.

The syntactical elements on which we will focus will be those of the European musical tradition, from the time of ancient Greece through the beginning of the 20th century.

We'll start with those aspects of the musical language that are most easily perceived by ear—timbre and meter—and from there, we'll move on to the more challenging syntactical elements of tonality and harmony. Lectures One through Three introduce the five basic categories of musical instruments—strings, woodwinds, brass, percussion, and keyboard instruments—and their individual timbral (sound) qualities. Lectures Four through Six explore the nature of beat, meter and tempo, including duple and triple meter, syncopation, compound meter, additive meter, and asymmetrical meter. We will also examine music that is not characterized by a regular meter. From Lecture Seven onward, we will examine tonality, beginning with its most basic aspects: pitches and the Pythagorean collection. We will explore pitch collections (modes), the major and minor modes, tuning systems, the anatomy and function of intervals, key relationships and the circle of fifths, melody, and functional tonality, including harmonic progressions, cadences, and modulation.

This Western musical language is a rich, varied, and magnificent one. It is a language that pays us back a hundredfold for every detail we come to recognize and perceive, and it is a language that will only get richer and more varied as our increasingly global culture contributes ever more vocabulary to it.

Lecture One
The Language of Music

Scope:

Music is a language, and like any language, its syntax is constantly changing. In order to deepen the experience of listening to music, we need to understand some basic syntactical elements, including timbre, meter, tonality, and harmony. This course begins by discussing the fundamental nature of the five basic classifications of musical instruments: strings, woodwinds, brass, percussion, and keyboard instruments. We will then look at some of the different techniques for producing a variety of sounds on string instruments.

Outline

I. The term *music theory* implies that there is a "science" of music, an all-encompassing set of truisms that, once understood, reveals the essence of music and establishes a set of rules that govern what composers can and cannot do as they create a piece of music.

    A. As such, the term *music theory* is misleading. We do not grasp musical syntax the way we grasp facts.

        1. Rather, we first learn to distinguish different sonic and temporal phenomena.

        2. Then, we come to understand how those phenomena are interrelated.

        3. After that, we can begin to understand how and why we perceive structural integrity and expressive meaning in any given section of music.

        4. Learning musical syntax is much like learning a language: We start with rudiments and gradually accumulate understanding as we comprehend that language in ever more sophisticated ways.

        5. Music is an art, not a science.

        6. What constitutes the art of music is a syntax that is constantly changing, based on the time, place, and aesthetic taste of a particular composer and the expressive *reason-to-be* of a particular piece of music.

    B. The goal of this course is to provide the intellectual tools and listening skills necessary to deepen immeasurably the experience of any music you might encounter, including concert music.

    1. The nature of this course precludes instruction in musical notation. We will not learn to read music, but this is a blessing in disguise, because we will, instead, learn to use our ears, an infinitely more useful skill than simply learning to recognize musical constructs on paper.

    2. Indeed, we will learn to build a musical vocabulary that includes timbre, meter, tonality, and harmony.

C. The course will focus on musical syntactical elements of the European musical tradition from ancient Greece through the 20th century.

D. Our working definition of music is "sound in time" or "time ordered by sound."

    1. When we talk about the *sound* aspect of music, we will be discussing everything from instruments and instrumental combinations to melody, harmony, texture, and tonality.

    2. When we talk about the *time* aspect of music, we will be discussing some aspect of rhythm.

II. We begin with that most easily perceived aspect of musical language, timbre: the physical sound produced by individual instruments and combinations of instruments. Instruments are classified by how they initiate and maintain their sound. There are five such major classifications.

A. Stringed instruments produce sound by bowing or plucking.

    1. Bowed stringed instruments are the most numerous in the modern orchestra.

    2. Plucked instruments include the harp and the guitar.

B. Woodwind, or wind, instruments initiate and maintain their sound when air is blown into a generally cylindrical instrument.

    1. Air may be blown directly through the instrument, as in the case of the piccolo and flute.

2. Air can be blown into the instrument indirectly, through a thin piece of cane called a *reed*, as in the case of the clarinet and saxophone families.

3. Air can also be blown indirectly into the instrument through two small reeds clamped together with a small space between them, as in the case of the double-reed instruments: oboe, English horn, and bassoon.

4. Not all woodwind instruments are made of wood, but the term was coined when they all, in fact, were. The metal flute, for example, did not become standard until the 1930s.

C. The brass instruments produce one of those miracles of sound that occurs when a flatulent burst of air goes through several feet of tubing to emerge mellow and only vaguely metallic in sound at the other end. **Trombone demonstration**.

D. Percussion instruments initiate and maintain their sound by striking, scraping, rattling, or mashing one object against another.

E. Keyboards constitute a problematic classification because, properly classified, the harpsichord would be a plucked string instrument, the piano would be a percussion instrument, and the organ would be a wind instrument.

F. In the 1970s and 1980s, a sixth instrumental category might have been added: electronics.

1. Electronics—synthesized sound—was once believed to be the wave of the future. But, as it turns out, the "wave" never happened.

2. Composers prefer to write music for real people playing real instruments, and audiences prefer to listen to this kind of music.

3. Ironically, digital electronics are used today to imitate those "antiquated" instruments they were supposed to replace.

III. The bowed stringed instruments are those of the violin family, which consists of four instruments.

A. The four instruments of the violin family have, collectively, a range of five octaves—the basic range of the human voice:

soprano, alto, tenor, and bass (SATB).

1. The violin is the soprano voice.

2. Perfected in workshops around Cremona, Italy, between approximately 1600 and 1750, the violin is capable of extraordinary lyricism, power, agility, nuance, and precision, as well as unworldly beauty. **Musical selection**: Johann Sebastian Bach, Partita no. 2 in D Minor for Solo Violin, BWV 1004 (c. 1720), Chaconne.

B. The viola corresponds to the alto voice.

1. The viola is slightly bigger than the violin and pitched a perfect fifth lower.

2. It has a softer, fuller sound than the violin. **Musical selection**: Robert Schumann, *Märchenbilder* for Viola and Piano, op. 113 (1851), movement 1.

C. Among the bowed strings, the violoncello ('cello, for short) is second only to the violin in terms of its lyric capabilities and range of nuance. It corresponds to the tenor voice. **Musical selection**: Johann Sebastian Bach, Suite no. 3 in C Major for Solo 'Cello, BWV 1009 (c. 1720), Bourrée.

D. While the violin and 'cello together constitute the foreground of the string choir, the bass, like the viola, generally plays a supportive or background role.

1. Because basses are less than ideal for playing thematic ideas, unless the composer wants a special effect, they are rarely given solos.

2. Among the most famous bass solos in the orchestral repertoire is the funereal version of *Frère Jacques* from Gustav Mahler's Symphony no. 1. **Musical selection**: Gustav Mahler, Symphony no. 1 in D Major (*Titan*, 1888), movement 3, opening.

IV. There are three generic groupings of instrumental genres.

A. A solo work is a composition for one instrument, exemplified by the partita and suite for 'cello by Bach that we just heard.

B. A chamber work is a composition for two or more instruments in which there is but one player per part, such as the *Märchenbilder* by Schumann.

C. An orchestral work is a composition for multiple instruments in which at least one part is doubled, meaning that two or more instruments are playing the same part (the same music).

1. Mahler's Symphony no. 1 is such a piece. For example, it calls for roughly 30 violinists divided into two parts: 16 first violinists and 14 second violinists.
2. The first violinists are all playing the same part. The same is true for the second violinists.

V. The violin family creates a homogenous, flexible, and non-fatiguing sound.

A. The violin family is the backbone of the orchestra.

B. The string quartet is the single most important chamber music combination. **Musical selection**: Wolfgang Mozart, String Quartet in Bb Major, K. 458 (*Hunt*, 1784), movement 1, opening.

C. A string quartet consists of two violins, a viola, and a 'cello, which play together as equal partners.

D. To appreciate the rich, homogenous sound of the violin family, we listen to the following excerpt. **Musical selection**: Peter Ilyich Tchaikovsky, Serenade for Strings in C Major, op. 48 (1875), movement 1.

E. Bowed instruments are capable of producing an incredible variety of different sounds.

1. Muted (*Con sordino*): Bowed strings can be muted using a small device (called a *mute*) that is clipped to the bridge of the instrument. In the following excerpt, the composer, Johannes Brahms, mutes the violins and 'cello in order to put the unmuted viola in high relief. **Musical selection**: Johannes Brahms, String Quartet no. 3 in Bb Major, op. 67 (1875), movement 3 (repeated).
2. *Sul tasto* ("on the fingerboard") creates a soft, flute-like sound by bowing over the fingerboard. This technique has a downside: The rosin put on the bow to help it grip the strings is spread on the fingerboard, where sooner or later, the string player will put his or her fingers.
3. *Sul ponticello* ("on the bridge") reduces the fundamental pitch almost to its overtones, creating a weird, "glassy" effect. This is stunningly illustrated at the end of

Beethoven's C-sharp (C#) Minor String Quartet. **Musical selection**: Ludwig van Beethoven, String Quartet in C# Minor, op. 131 (1826), movement 5 (repeated).

4. *Col legno* ("with the wood") requires players to flip their bows over and use the wooden side to play the strings, producing little pitch, but, rather, a "clicking" sound, especially if the composer indicates *col legno battuto*, meaning that the bow must bounce off the strings. **Musical selection**: Hector Berlioz, *Symphonie fantastique* (1830), movement 5 (repeated). This technique can scratch and even chip the bow, which can be as valuable as the instrument itself.

5. *Pizzicato* ("plucked") is a very common technique involving plucked strings. There are various types of pizzicati, of which the most common is to pluck the string with the fleshy part of the finger. A more brittle effect can be obtained by plucking with the fingernail. A percussive effect can be obtained when the string is pulled back so far that, when released, it snaps against the fingerboard. This is called a *snap*, or *Bartok* pizzicato. The most common type of pizzicato is illustrated in the following excerpt. **Musical selection**: Peter Ilyich Tchaikovsky, Symphony no. 4 in F Minor, op. 36 (1877), movement 3 ("Scherzo Pizzicato"), opening.

Lecture One—Transcript
The Language of Music

This is Lecture One and it is entitled "The Language of Music." Yes, the musical language. Music theory. You will forgive me for turning, as I always do in moments of intellectual want, to my Webster's Collegiate Dictionary, which defines the word *theory* as, and we quote: "The analysis of a set of facts in their relation to one another." [Webster's Seventh New Collegiate Dictionary]

My friends, few words offer as much rational solace as does the word *theory*. Examining the plausibility of a theory demands that we analyze facts, reason logically, think objectively, and examine comprehensively. Having done so, we will—assumably—arrive at a conclusion that is the end product of a process of scientific method, which is itself defined as: "Principle and procedures for the systematic pursuit of knowledge involving the recognition and formulation of a problem, the collection of data through observation and experiment, and the formulation and testing of hypotheses." [Webster's Seventh New Collegiate Dictionary, 771] Ergo: If something is a theory, it is knowable; it's something we can study, it's something we can learn, it's something that is explicable and rational. The theory of relativity, the theory of evolution, game theory: complex, yes, but concepts that can be understood, compartmentalized, absorbed and digested.

Music theory. Implied in that compact and oh-so-innocent-sounding phrase is the idea that there is a knowable, graspable, all-encompassing set of truisms that once understood, compartmentalized, absorbed and digested, the very essence of music will stand revealed, its various elements and expressive content united into a singularity, the whole greater than the sum of its parts. Wrong. Speaking for myself, I dislike the phrase *music theory* almost as much as I dislike the phrase *music appreciation*. What we call *theory*, what we call *music theory*, is in reality a huge and varied syntax, a syntax that deals with the various ways sounds can be arrayed across time to create a musical experience.

We don't "grasp" musical syntax the way we grasp facts and the analysis of facts; rather, we first learn to distinguish different sonic and temporal phenomena; then we come to understand how those phenomena are interrelated; after which we can begin to understand how and why we perceive structural integrity and expressive meaning in a given section of music. Learning musical syntax is very much like learning a language: We start with the rudiments and ever so slowly accumulate understanding and insight as we comprehend that language in ever more sophisticated ways.

The phrase *music theory* would imply that there is a science of music, a set of rules and regulations, of absolute rights and wrongs, that govern what composers can and cannot do as they create a piece of music. Wrong again. In reality, music theory, like music itself, is an art and not a science, something much more akin to language (with all its idiosyncrasies, quirks, eccentricities, and inexplicable idioms) than it is a body of "knowledge covering general truths or the operation of general laws especially as obtained and tested through scientific method," which is how my "WebCol" defines science. The point of this introductory screed: Let's think of those aspects of music theory that we're about to study—timbre, meter, tonality, harmony, and so forth—not as a body of truths and laws, but, rather, as a constantly evolving and variable syntax.

What This Course Is and Isn't and What We Can Expect to Accomplish in 16 Lectures!

My friends, in any high school, college, or conservatory music theory course, the first prerequisite is the ability to read music. This makes absolute sense. If we're going to study the syntax of any language, then we need to be able to read that language! Would any of us contemplate taking a course on the syntax of the English language without first being able to read? Well, of course not. And yet, the limitation of a non-interactive course like this one is that it cannot teach the intricacies of music notation, and therefore it cannot provide a notationally (and therefore visually) based exploration of music theory. Well, to tell you the truth, our limits are a blessing in disguise!

Now, before you begin packing this course up to return for a full refund, I would explain from both a philosophical and practical point of view how this course is going to work, what you're going to get out of it, and on what pedagogic precedents it rests.

Philosophically, my Teaching Company courses have always assumed that the attentive listener can perceive and understand pretty much anything, provided we know what to listen for and provided we listen carefully and intelligently.

Given the nature of a course like this, I cannot teach you how to read and write music. But, I can teach you to hear and identify those aspects of the musical language that are, collectively, the means to comprehending—on a fairly intimate level—the music of the Western repertoire and, to a not-insignificant degree, the music of many other world cultures as well.

And thus, the essential goal of this course: to provide you with the intellectual tools and listening skills necessary to deepen immeasurably the experience of, one, my other teaching company courses, and two, pretty much any music you might encounter, be it concert music, popular music, jazz, rock & roll, whatever.

The pedagogical precedents on which this course rests are those foreign language teaching methods that present a language as an integrated whole through conversation. Yes, we're all aware that if we want to master a language, we will, sooner or later, have to resort to workbooks, conjugation exercises, vocabulary lists, and the like, just as if we want to master the art of music, an intense and extended notation-based course of study will, sooner or later, be required.

But, I would state the obvious: we must crawl before we can luge, and walk before we can surf, and obviously, we all learned our native language by ear before we learned to read it. So this course is about using our ears, about discovering and exploring musical syntax through our ears, by learning what the parts of the musical language sound like, rather than what they look like on paper. We'll start with those aspects of the musical language that are most easily perceived by ear—timbre and meter—and from there we'll move on to the more challenging syntactical elements of tonality and harmony.

An important point, to be made upfront: The syntactical elements on which we will focus will be those of the European musical tradition, from the time of ancient Greece through the 20th century. We make no apology for this; there's just so much that can be covered in 16 lectures!

Music as a Language

The reason why we can teach music as a language is because music *is* a language. It is a mode of sonic communication through which a tremendous amount of information of all sorts—aesthetic, stylistic, emotional, and so forth—can be transferred with an ease that belies its complexity. The cliché that music is the international language may be tiresome, but it is accurate. I would suggest that music is the ultimate language, a mega-language, a language in which our hard-wired proclivities to use successions of pitches and sounds to communicate are exaggerated, intensified, and codified into a sonic experience capable of infinitely more expressive depth and nuance than mere words alone.

Music—a Guiding Definition

Before we begin to listen, we've one more vital task and that is to actually define music, a discussion that could positively finish off this lecture and the next, given how many different ways music has been defined across the span of recorded history. In lieu of such a potentially tiresome discussion, we'll want a definition of music that includes pretty much everything and excludes pretty much nothing: a definition that will provide a starting point for our exploration of the musical language, of music theory. But, before we offer our definition of music, I would present to you a couple of traditional definitions.

The dictionary defines music as: "the science or art of incorporating intelligible combinations of tones into a composition having structure and continuity." [Webster's Seventh New Collegiate Dictionary, 558] My friends, there's so much wrong with that definition that it's hard to know where to begin. For example, who's to determine what constitutes an "intelligible combination of tones" from an unintelligible combination of tones? And what about drum music, an entire repertoire that doesn't use tones (meaning individual pitches) at all? Then, there's the phrase about combining tones "into a composition," a phrase that would, by definition, exclude improvisation and most oral tradition and folk musics. And the last phrase of the definition, that music is the art of combining tones "into a composition having structure and continuity"? Yes, much music displays a perceivable structure and continuity, but you know what, much does not. All in all, that's as useless a definition of music as I've ever heard, or read, and I do wish the good folks at Merriam Webster had consulted me before they printed it.

We turn next to the great mid-twentieth century composer, Roger Sessions, who was the teacher of my teacher, a gentleman named Andrew Imbrie. Sessions defined music as: "controlled movement of sound in time." Better, although we respectfully ask, controlled by whom? Our working definition of music will draw on what is best in Sessions' definition: Music is sound in time, or, if you prefer, time ordered by sound. That's it, and that's enough. That definition isolates the two essential aspects of music—sound and time—without any qualifications. It's a definition we can most comfortably live with.

When we talk about the sound aspect of music, we'll be discussing everything from instruments and instrumental combinations to melody, harmony, texture, and tonality. When we talk about the time aspect of music, we'll be talking about some aspect of rhythm. We begin with that most accessible, most easily perceived sound aspect of the music language: timbre.

Timbre: Part 1

Timbre—spelled t-i-m-b-r-e—refers to the actual, physical sound, or tone color, produced by individual instruments and/or combinations of instruments. If music is a language, and indeed it is, then musical instruments—singly and collectively—are the "voice" of that language. We are going to spend the remainder of this lecture and Lectures Two and Three discussing this most accessible aspect of the musical language. Along the way, we will build a vocabulary for addressing other sound aspects of music, with sidebars on instrumental genres, dynamics, transposing instruments, and the evolving nature of the orchestra.

In the Beginning

Yes, in the beginning, there was the human voice, and, excepting the tortuous, canine-like ululations of certain high-profile pop-singers, the voice is good. It is trite but true to say that most music, like language itself, springs from the voice. As we are all generally familiar with the sound of the human voice, we will move directly forward to the sounds of Western orchestral instruments. However, let us always be aware that most musical instruments aspire to the flexibility, the lyricism, and to the expressive power of the human voice.

Instrumental Classifications

Instruments are classified by how they initiate and maintain their sound. Aside from the human voice, there are five major classifications, or families, of instruments in the Western musical tradition. One at a time.

Instrumental classification number one: stringed instruments, which initiate their sound by being either bowed, or plucked. Bowed stringed instruments, the most numerous instruments in the modern orchestra (for reasons we'll discuss in a moment), most commonly initiate and maintain their sound by rubbing a bow against a string. Plucked stringed instruments, like the guitar and harp, initiate their sound by plucking a string.

Instrumental classification number two: The woodwind, or wind instruments, initiate and maintain their sound by blowing air into a generally cylindrical instrument, either directly, in the case of the piccolo and flute, or through a thin piece of cane called a reed, as in the case of the clarinet and saxophone families, or through two very small reeds clamped together with a small space in between them, the so-called double-reed instruments: the oboe, English horn, and bassoon. One might wonder why these instruments are collectively referred to as the woodwinds when, in fact, they are not all made out of wood—for example, the flute. The answer: Well, when the term was invented, they were indeed all, including the flute, made out of wood. The fully metal flute didn't become standard until the 1930s, long after the term *woodwind* was coined and in common use.

Instrumental classification number three: the brass instruments. We observe, ever so quickly, but with great reverence, a few of nature's miracles: the miracle of birth; the existence of love; the Northern California coastline. The fact that when the brutally flatulent sound of a Bronx cheer [**Demonstration**] is passed first through a cupped mouthpiece [**Trombone demonstration**] and then through several feet of metal tubing, the sound that emerges is no longer flatulent, but, rather, sweet, mellow, and only vaguely metallic in sound.

[**Trombone demonstration**] As you can tell, my trombone-playing days are far behind me. But, that doesn't change the fact that brass instruments are a miracle of nature!

Instrumental classification number four: percussion instruments. Percussion instruments initiate and maintain their sounds by striking, scraping, rattling, or mashing one object against another.

Instrumental classification number five: keyboards. Now, this is a problematic classification, because properly classified, a harpsichord would be a plucked string instrument, the piano a percussion instrument, and the organ a wind instrument. For now, let's just group them together and avoid the certifiably Talmudic discussion regarding their classification. Thank you on this one.

If this course had been written back in the 1970s or 1980s, it would have included a sixth instrumental category: electronics. There was a genuine belief back then that digitally synthesized sound was the wave of the future, and that an entirely new vocabulary of sound, one relevant to the technocracy of the modern world, was just around the corner. You know what? It never happened. As it turned out, composers prefer to write for real people playing real instruments, and audiences would rather listen to real people playing real instruments. Ironically, more than anything else, digital electronics are used today to imitate those "antiquated" instruments that they were purportedly going to replace!

One by one, let's examine the instrumental families that make up our classifications, beginning with the bowed strings.

Bowed Strings—The Violin Family

The violin family consists of four instruments, which together span a range of over five octaves. The four instruments of the violin family correspond to the four basic ranges of the human voice: soprano, alto, tenor and bass (what's referred to in shorthand as SATB). The violin is the soprano voice; the viola the alto voice, the violoncello (or 'cello for short) the tenor voice, and the contra, or double bass, the bass voice.

If all instruments (excepting the percussion) aspire to the condition of the human voice, well, then it is the violin that gets closest to that condition. Perfected in workshops in and around Cremona, Italy, between roughly 1600 and 1750, the violin is capable of an extraordinary degree of lyricism, power, agility, nuance, precision, and sheer unworldly beauty. It is, without any doubt, one of the great creations of our species. As an example, let's hear the beginning of Johann Sebastian Bach's Chaconne in D Minor for solo violin, from his Partita no. 2 in D Minor of circa 1720. It's an amazing work, in which every one of the violin's lyric and dramatic capabilities are pushed to the limit. [**Musical selection:** Johann Sebastian Bach, Partita no. 2 in D Minor, BWV 1004 (c. 1720), Chaconne]

The viola is two to three inches longer than the violin, and is pitched a perfect fifth (that's five white keys on a piano) lower than the violin. The viola's got a softer, fuller, somewhat less-focused tone than the violin, and, more often than not, it plays an accompanimental role to the violin. As an example of the rich, husky voice of the viola, let's hear a bit of the first movement of Robert Schumann's *Märchenbilder* for Viola and Piano of 1851. [**Musical selection:** Robert Schumann, *Märchenbilder* for Viola and Piano, op. 113 (1851), movement 1]

Among the bowed strings, the 'cello is second only to the violin in terms of its lyric capabilities. And really, my friends, is there a sexier instrument in all the orchestra, with its deep, resonant, throaty tone, and its frankly voluptuous shape, resting comfortably between its performer's knees? We think not. We sample the Bourrée from Bach's Suite for Solo 'Cello no. 3, of circa 1720. [**Musical selection:** Johann Sebastian Bach, Suite no. 3 in C Major for Solo 'Cello, BWV 1009 (c. 1720), Bourrée]

If the violin and 'cello together constitute the foreground of the string choir—those instruments most likely to be given a principal melody line, or theme—then the double bass, like the viola, generally plays a supportive, or background role. Where the viola typically provides middle support by supplying countermelodies and filling in harmonies, the bass provides the foundation for the entire orchestra, as the bass line and the harmonies underlain by the bass line govern the other, higher instrumental parts. The basses are big instruments, often over six feet tall, with a big, powerful, if rather ponderous sound, perfect for providing an underpinning, but unless a composer wants to create a particular effect, less-than-ideal for playing thematic ideas. As such, my friends, the basses are rarely given solos in orchestral music. Perhaps the single most famous orchestral bass solo is the opening of the third movement of Gustav Mahler's Symphony no. 1 of 1888. The movement begins with a dark, ominous, funereal, absolutely whacko version of the round *Frère Jacques*, a tune Mahler knew as *Bruder Martin*, as played by a solo bass. [**Musical selection:** Gustav Mahler, Symphony no. 1 in D Major (*Titan*, 1888), movement 3, opening]

Sidebar—Instrumental Genres

We interrupt this regularly scheduled examination of Western musical instruments to broach the subject of instrumental genres. An instrumental genre is a particular grouping of instruments. There are three generic instrumental groupings with which we should be familiar: solo, chamber, and orchestral. A solo work is a composition for one instrument and one instrument only, like the Bach violin partita and 'cello suite we just sampled. A chamber work is a composition for two or more instruments in which there is but one player per part, like the movement from Robert Schumann's *Märchenbilder* for Viola and Piano that we also just sampled. An orchestral work is a composition for multiple instruments in which at least one part is doubled, meaning that two or more instruments play the same part, the same music, at the same time. For example, Gustav Mahler's Symphony no. 1, of which we just heard the beginning of the third movement, calls for around 30 violinists, divided into two parts: 16 first violinists and 14 second violinists. Those 16 first violinists are all playing the same part; the same is true for the second violinists. We say, then, that the first and second violin parts are doubled, and any such doubling would qualify a work as being orchestral. Exit sidebar!

Back, Please, to the Bowed Strings

The violin family creates a homogeneous and non-fatiguing sound from top to bottom, and for that reason it has been the backbone of the orchestra since the orchestra came into existence in the 17th century. When we say non-fatiguing, we mean that we're willing and able to listen to bowed strings play for indefinite lengths of time. As opposed to a piccolo ensemble, which would almost instantly induce both bleeding and hysteria.

Just as the strings are by far the most numerous instruments in the orchestra, so the string quartet—an ensemble consisting of two violins, a viola, and a 'cello—has been, almost from the moment of its invention around 1750, the single most important and prestigious chamber music combination. Let's listen, please, to a string quartet, and let's be aware of the blend—the rich homogeneity of its sound—from top to bottom. Mozart, String Quartet in B-flat [Bb] Major, *The Hunt*, movement one, opening! [**Musical selection:** Wolfgang Mozart, String Quartet in Bb Major, K. 458 (*Hunt*, 1784), movement 1, opening]

To answer the question: Why does a string quartet consist of two violins, a viola, and a 'cello, and not a violin, viola, 'cello, and a bass? Well, there are two reasons. One: At the time the string quartet was born, the bass, as we know it, had not yet developed. Two: Even if it had already existed, the bass would still not have been an appropriate instrument for a string quartet. You see, by its very nature, the string quartet assumes that each of its four constituent instrumental voices will be an equal player in the development of the music. The bass is neither supple nor agile enough to be able to participate, on equal terms, in the four-part conversation that is, by definition, a string quartet.

Now, talk about a rich, homogeneous sound. Let's now sample a string orchestra, an orchestra consisting of, simply, first violins, second violins, violas, 'cellos, and basses. We're going to hear the first-movement introduction to Peter Ilyich Tchaikovsky's glorious Serenade for Strings of 1875. In my humble opinion, there is not a more lush, more goose-bump inducing sound on this planet than that of a string orchestra. [**Musical selection:** Peter Ilyich Tchaikovsky, Serenade for Strings in C Major, op. 48 (1875), movement 1]

Bowed Strings Gone Wild!

Bowed stringed instruments are capable of producing an incredible variety of different sounds. Because we must, let's sample some of that variety!

Con Sordino (With a Mute)

Bowed strings can be muted by clipping a small, comb-like device to the bridge of the instrument, which muffles and darkens the sound by reducing the amount of vibration transferred from the strings to the body of the instrument. Composers will mute the strings for various reasons: sometimes for the mood of quiet intimacy that muting creates and sometimes to highlight a non-muted instrument. As an example of the latter, we turn to the third movement of Johannes Brahms's String Quartet no. 3 of 1875. Brahms marks the movement *agitato* (agitated) and he turns the thematic duties over to the viola. Brahms, aware that the viola could very well be drowned out by the other instruments, mutes the violins and 'cello, thereby putting the unmuted viola in high relief. [**Musical selection:** Johannes Brahms, String Quartet no. 3 in Bb Major, op. 67 (1875), movement 3] That was a short excerpt. I know we want to hear it again. So, let's hear that again. [**Musical selection:** Johannes Brahms, String Quartet no. 3 in Bb Major, op. 67 (1875), movement 3]

Sul Tasto and Sul Ponticello

Another way of changing the tone color of a bowed string instrument is to ask the player to bow over the fingerboard, called *sul tasto*, meaning, literally, "on the fingerboard," or ask them to bow near the bridge, called *sul ponticello*, meaning, literally, "on the bridge."

Bowing over the fingerboard (sul tasto) creates a soft, flute-like sound, not unlike that created by using a mute. However, it takes a few seconds for a mute to be put on, or taken off, whereas sul tasto can be effected instantly, merely by bowing higher up on the string. Now, you'd think that composers would use sul tasto all the time, instead of the mute, except for one thing: String players really dislike playing sul tasto. You see, in order to make their horse-hair bows grip the strings, string players rub the bows with rosin. When you play sul tasto, you inevitably get rosin on a part of the string where, sooner or later, you're going to have to put your fingers. Ergo, rosin on the fingers. Rightfully, string players hate having rosin on their fingers; it's like putting Velcro on the blade of an ice skate.

Now, as a composer, you can insist that a recalcitrant string player play sul tasto, but she won't like you for it, and by association, she won't like your piece. The player might even decide that a bad performance is a necessary inevitability, given your insensitivity towards her and her instrument: "Oh, sorry about all the wrong notes, but I couldn't help it because of all the rosin on my fingers."

Bowing near the bridge—what's called *sul ponticello*—reduces to almost nothing the fundamental pitch, leaving only its overtones to be heard. Oh, it's a killer effect, and it produces a weird, glassy, fingernails-on-the-blackboard sort of sound. Such a moment occurs near the conclusion of the fifth movement of Beethoven's String Quartet in C-sharp [C#] Minor, op. 131 of 1826. Our excerpt will begin with a series of plucked, or pizzicato notes, followed by the strings playing sul ponticello, after which the players will move their bows back to a normal bowing position. Let's hear this amazing change of timbre, then, from sul ponticello back to *modo ordinario*, or "ordinary position." [**Musical selection:** Ludwig van Beethoven, String Quartet in C# Minor, op. 131 (1826), movement 5.] It's an extraordinary effect and how a clinically deaf composer thought of using it we can't know. But, we must hear it again! [**Musical selection:** Ludwig van Beethoven, String Quartet in C# Minor, op. 131 (1826), movement 5]

Col Legno

Col legno is another fabulous string technique, though like sul tasto, composers should use it sparingly and judiciously! *Col legno* means, literally, "with the wood," meaning that the players flip their bows over and use the wooden side of the bow to play the strings. Now, we won't hear much pitch in a col legno passage, but we'll hear lots of clicking, especially if the composer indicates the passage is to be played *col legno battuto*, meaning that the players actually bounce the wooden side of the bow on the string, as Hector Berlioz indicates should be done during this following passage in the fifth and final movement of his *Symphonie fantastique* of 1830. [**Musical selection:** Hector Berlioz, *Symphonie fantastique* (1830), movement 5] Oh, too good! Let's, please, hear that again! [**Musical selection:** Hector Berlioz, *Symphonie fantastique* (1830), movement 5] Great as that sounds, string players dislike playing col legno even more than they do sul tasto! And again, who can blame them? Playing col legno can scratch and even chip the varnish on their bows, bows that are often as valuable as the instruments themselves! String players will usually carry with them a backup, or junk bow, for just such occasions.

Pizzicato

Pizzicato means "to pluck the strings." It's a very common technique, and there are various sorts of pizzicati: You can pluck the string with the fleshy part of the finger, which is the most common type. You can pluck with your fingernail in order to get a more brittle effect, or you can pull the string so far back that when it's released it snaps against the fingerboard, creating a percussive effect, something called a *snap*, or *Bartok*, pizzicato. Let's hear some garden-variety, finger pizzicati: the opening section of the third movement of Tchaikovsky's Symphony no. 4 of 1877. No mystery regarding what we're about to hear, as Tchaikovsky entitles the movement "Scherzo Pizzicato." [**Musical selection:** Peter Ilyich Tchaikovsky, Symphony no. 4 in F Minor, op. 36 (1877), movement 3, opening] When we return, our exploration of instrumental timbre continues! Thank you.

Lecture Two
Timbre, Continued

Scope:

We continue our exploration of timbre with plucked instruments and wind instruments. Most wind instruments are part of an extended family and, excepting the flute family, use one or two reeds to produce their sound. Double-reed instruments include the oboe, English horn, bassoon, and contrabassoon. Single-reed instruments include the clarinet and saxophone families. This lecture also discusses the concepts of transposing instruments and dynamics.

Outline

I. Our exploration of timbre continues with the plucked strings.
    A. In the following example, there are three primary instrumental timbres: flute, harp, and string orchestra. **Musical selection**: Wolfgang Mozart, Concerto in C Major for Flute and Harp, K. 299 (1788), movement 2.
    B. The harp is the ancestral instrument of both the harpsichord and the piano.
    C. The harp is the only modern orchestral instrument that is of western European origin—of Celtic origin.

II. Virtually every modern type of wind instrument is part of an extended SATB (soprano, alto, tenor, bass) family of instruments.
    A. The most commonly heard instruments of the flute family are the piccolo and the flute. Despite its small size, the piccolo has a piercing sound. **Musical selection**: John Philip Sousa, *The Stars and Stripes Forever* (1896).
    B. The double-reed instruments—oboe, English horn, bassoon, and contrabassoon—are very difficult to play because of the mouthpiece, which consists of two tiny pieces of cane, bound together, leaving an extremely small space between them. This requires a player to use a lot of force to blow into the instrument.

1. The oboe (meaning, literally, "high wood") produces a nasal, piercing quality of sound that makes it ideal for tuning the other instruments in the orchestra before a performance.
2. The oboe family consists of the oboe, English horn, oboe d'amore, baritone oboe, and heckelphone, or bass oboe. The last three instruments are not, today, considered standard orchestral instruments.
3. The alto instrument of the double-reed family is the English horn, pitched five scale-steps below the oboe. The English horn is neither of English origin nor a horn. It and the oboe evolved from the ancient shawm. Both the oboe and English horn evoke the sort of pastoral melancholy associated with their ancestral shawm. **Musical selection**: Hector Berlioz, *Symphonie fantastique* (1830), movement 3, opening.
4. The bassoon is dark and heavy in its lower register; clear and sonorous in its middle register; reedy and intense in its upper register; and lyric, penetrating, and flexible in all its registers. The following excerpt illustrates the bassoon's upper register. **Musical selection**: Igor Stravinsky, *The Rite of Spring* (1912), opening.
5. The contra or double bassoon is folded over itself several times. It is the lowest instrument in the orchestra and provides the foundation for the entire woodwind section. **Musical selection**: Wolfgang Mozart, Sonata in Bb Major for Bassoon and 'Cello, K. 292/K. 196c (1775, arranged for two contrabassoons), opening.

C. In the single-reed family, there are 10 clarinets that are currently in use:
1. Soprano clarinet in A-flat (Ab)
2. Soprano clarinet in E-flat (Eb)
3. Clarinet in C
4. Clarinet in B-flat (Bb—the "standard" clarinet)
5. Clarinet in A
6. Alto clarinet in E-flat (Eb)
7. Basset horn in F
8. Bass clarinet in B-flat (Bb)
9. Contra-alto clarinet in E-flat (Eb)

10. Contrabass clarinet in B-flat (Bb)

D. All or nearly all of these instruments may be heard in a concert band or big marching band. For the purposes of orchestral music, three members of the clarinet family are commonly used: the soprano clarinet in Eb, the "standard" Bb clarinet, and the bass clarinet in Bb.

III. The key designations indicate that these instruments are *transposing instruments*. This means that their notated pitches are different from the sounded pitches.

A. Most instruments, for example, keyboards and strings, are in C, meaning that they are non-transposing instruments in concert pitch: When a player sees C written on a page of music, she plays a C on her instrument, and the pitch that sounds is called a *concert C*.

B. But this is not the case for transposing instruments.

1. The reason lies with the fingering. By using virtually the same fingering system, a musician can play all the instruments in a particular family of instruments.

2. When the pitch of C is played on an oboe, it sounds as a C. But because the English horn is longer than the oboe, the same fingering that produces the sound of C on the oboe actually produces the sound of F on the English horn.

3. For the English horn to play in the key of C, its part is notated five steps higher than C—in the key of G. It will then sound five steps lower—in the key of concert C.

4. The score of a work written for both transposing and non-transposing instruments will contain any number of different key signatures.

IV. All clarinets are single-reed instruments.

A. A single-reed instrument employs a wide, thin piece of cane fitted against a mouthpiece called a *beak*. The wide reed allows clarinetists to make their instruments sing with a nuance, flexibility, and vocality equaled only by the violin and the 'cello.

B. The following excerpt demonstrates the special qualities of the Bb clarinet's three registers: the rich warmth of its low, or *chalumeau*, register; the round mellowness of its middle register; and the gentle, almost flute-like sweetness of its upper, or *clarino*, register. **Musical selection**: Johannes Brahms, Quintet in B Minor for Clarinet and Strings, op. 115 (1891), movement 1, opening.

C. The sopranino clarinet in Eb, while not commonly heard, is nevertheless, heard often enough that it deserves to be demonstrated here.

   1. It has a shrill and piercing timbre.

   2. This quality suits it perfectly to its role in Hector Berlioz's *Symphonie fantastique*, where it represents a gnarled and evil witch who dances an obscene jig at a funeral. **Musical selection**: Hector Berlioz, *Symphonie fantastique* (1830), movement 5, sopranino clarinet solo.

   3. Berlioz was the most innovative orchestrator to his time. His use of instruments and instrumental combinations became a model for every generation that followed him, and his *Treatise on Orchestration* has been considered mandatory reading for composers and conductors since its original publication in 1843.

D. The bass clarinet in Bb combines the vocality and agility of a clarinet with the range of a Russian basso singer. **Musical selection**: Johann Sebastian Bach, Partita no. 2 in D Minor for Solo Violin, BWV 1004 (c. 1720), Chaconne, arranged for bass clarinet.

E. The saxophone family, which was invented by Adolphe Sax for use in 19th-century French military bands, has found its true niche in jazz. Like clarinets, saxophones employ a single reed.

V. The wind quintet is the preeminent chamber combination involving wind instruments.

A. The standard wind quintet consists of a flute, oboe, clarinet, bassoon, and French horn.

B. Although a brass instrument, the French horn is as timbrally comfortable in the company of wind instruments as it is among brass.

C. What makes a wind quintet so special for the listener and such a challenge for the composer is its amazing variety of instrumental timbres among the individual instruments and in combinations. In this, it is the polar opposite of a string quartet, which is about the blend of homogeneous instruments drawn from the same instrumental family. The challenge for the composer is to unite the wind quintet's rainbow of timbres into a timbral whole. **Musical selection**: Carl Nielsen, Quintet for Winds, op. 43 (1922), movement 4, opening.

VI. There are two categories of dynamics: fixed and graded.

    A. A fixed dynamic marking indicates a single, unchanging level of volume until another dynamic marking appears to change it.

        1. Fixed dynamics are arrayed around the two polarities of loud (*forte*) and soft (*piano*). **Piano example**: Ludwig van Beethoven, Piano Sonata no. 8 in C Minor, op. 13 (*Pathétique*, 1798), opening chords, marked *forte* and *piano*.

        2. These dynamics are subject to individual interpretation. **Piano examples**.

        3. *Moderately loud* is indicated by the marking *mf* (*mezzo-forte*).

        4. *Moderately soft* is indicated by the marking *mp* (*mezzo piano*).

        5. *Very loud* is identified by the Italian superlative *fortissimo* (*ff*) or *fortississimo* (*fff*).

        6. *Very soft* is identified as *pianissimo* (*pp*) or *pianississimo* (*ppp*).

    B. Graded dynamic markings are those used to indicate a progressive increase in loudness or softness, respectively, *crescendo* or *decrescendo* (*diminuendo*). On a page of music, the marking looks like a hairpin, either expanding to the right for a crescendo or gradually contracting to the right for a decrescendo.

Lecture Two—Transcript
Timbre, Continued

This is Lecture Two and it is entitled "Timbre, Continued." Please, my friends, some review. The phrase *music theory* is a misnomer. It implies that there is a rationally explicable, scientific basis to music. This is only partially true and we will discuss the acoustical bases of Western music in Lectures Seven and Eight when we tackle the subject of the overtone series. But, precisely how the overtone series has manifested itself in the instruments, pitch collections, or scales, melodies, harmonic systems, and historical styles of Western music is entirely cultural, cultural phenomena that together constitute the syntax of a varied, complex and extremely flexible language.

Our approach to this *language of music* is an admittedly limited one, since the nature of a course like this one precludes me from teaching and using musical notation. But, as we discussed in Lecture One, this is a blessing in disguise, because it forces us to use our ears. Learning to perceive the musical syntax with our ears is an infinitely more useful skill than simply learning to recognize musical constructs on paper. With our eyes? No. Better to be able to hear what we want to hear. With our ears thus properly informed, we can apply what we've learned to almost any piece of music in almost any style. Oh, I just love books and workbooks on music history and theory that are filled with charts and music notation and photos of musical instruments, but, because of the limits imposed by their medium, not a note of music is actually heard! That's like a cooking class without food, or a wine tasting without wine: It is a waste of time. A picture might be worth a thousand words, but when it comes to music, a musical excerpt is worth a thousand pictures! On this, you may quote me! We return to our exploration of timbre—instruments and instrumental color—that sonic element that gives voice to the musical language.

Plucked Strings

There is no more ancient and enduring family of musical instruments than the plucked strings. From the lyre of Orpheus to Jimi Hendrix's Fender Stratocaster, plucked string instruments have, for thousands of years, been the portable instruments of choice for bards, troubadours, minstrels, and rockers, not to mention those idealized angels in heaven, who sure as heck aren't playing trombones! Speaking of angels in heaven, let's hear a bit of the slow movement of Mozart's Concerto for Flute and Harp of 1778. While we listen to this excerpt, let's be aware of its three primary instrumental timbres, and how magically these timbres contrast and combine: the sweet, pure, sustained sound of the flute, the glowing, magical, plucked sound of the harp, and the smooth, homogeneous sound of the string orchestra in the accompaniment. [**Musical selection:** Wolfgang Mozart, Concerto in C Major for Flute and Harp, K. 299 (1778), movement 2] I would suggest that the magic of that music springs from two sources. One is from Mozart's imagination. The man couldn't write a bad piece of music even if you held a gun to his schnauzer's head. The second source of the magic lies with the instruments themselves: the amazing, almost unworldly combination of instrumental timbres that Mozart employs and how he combines and contrasts those timbres.

Two harp-oriented tidbits before we move on. One: The harp is the ancestral instrument of both the harpsichord and the piano. Remember that next time someone demeans the harp by referring to it as ear candy, or as a bouquet instrument, as it often is. Second: The harp is the answer to a great trivia question: name the only modern orchestral instrument that is of western European origin. Yup, it's the harp, which in its present form evolved from a Celtic instrument. That's right. The violin family, the brass, and woodwind instruments all evolved from Middle Eastern, Central Asian, or North African ancestors. Well, who would have thought!

The Woodwinds

Virtually every modern type of wind instrument is part of an extended, SATB, or soprano-alto-tenor-bass family of instruments. For example, from high-to-low, the flute family consists of the piccolo, the standard flute (which we just heard), an alto flute and a bass flute, the latter being a mammoth instrument that requires lungs the size of foundry bellows to play. The double-reed family consists of the standard oboe, the English horn, the bassoon, and the contrabassoon. Finally, the clarinet family consists of the sopranino clarinet, the familiar soprano clarinet in Bb, an alto clarinet and a bass clarinet. One at a time.

The Flute Family

The standard flute is, like the violin, an instrument capable of astonishing clarity, agility, and brilliance. The other most commonly heard member of the flute family is the piccolo, the full name of which is *flauto piccolo*. It's Italian for "little flute." Yes, small it is, but don't ever, ever let its size fool you. A piccolo in the hands of a professional can bleed you like no other instrument this side of the scalpel, which is, I might point out, rather small as well!

(Oh, I must tell you a true story. My wife is a professional flute player who specializes on the piccolo. After we moved in together, I had the opportunity to hear her practice the piccolo for the first time. Despite the fact that she was downstairs at one end of the house and I was upstairs at the other end of the house, the intensity of the sound was, well, it was excruciating; I could feel it in my teeth; behind my eyes, in my knees. So I went downstairs to the room in which she was practicing. She put down her piccolo. I asked, "How can you play that thing and not go deaf?" She said, "Huh?" I began to ask the question for a second time when she popped the earplugs out of her ears. Just like that, she'd answered my question. Piccolo players wear ear plugs to protect themselves from their own instruments. Sadly, the rest of us are not usually so equipped. Just wanted to share that with you.)

For sheer piercing power and brilliance, the upper octave of a piccolo cannot be covered by any sound on this planet excepting perhaps a large-scale volcanic eruption, and even that's a maybe. And while the piccolo is often used to reinforce the flute, or the violins, it's at its best when it's cut free to do its own thing, soaring above the band and demonstrating an agility that is second-to-no-other instrument. As an example, let's hear what just has to be the most famous piccolo solo in the repertoire, the stratospheric piccolo obbligato from John Philip Sousa's *The Stars and Stripes Forever* of 1896. [**Musical selection:** John Philip Sousa, *The Stars and Stripes Forever* (1896)]

The Double Reed Family

The double reed instruments—the oboe, English horn, bassoon and contrabassoon—are really, really hard to play. The mouthpiece consists of two tiny pieces of cane that are bound together in such a way as to leave an extremely small space between them. In order to get the two reeds to vibrate together, you must grasp this tiny mouthpiece tightly between your lips and blow for all you're worth. You blow until your eyes begin to bulge, until your nasal passages inflate like balloons, and your brain get pushed back against your skull case. Migraines? Blurred vision? Hey, they come with the territory, my friends. Double reed players learn to play through the pain. Pain. It's a word often associated with the personalities of oboe players in particular, no disrespect intended! It is, however, one of those chicken-or-egg questions: Are overly fastidious, anal-retentive people attracted to the oboe because of its technical difficulty and its nasal, arguably whiny sound, or do the technical demands and the sound of the oboe turn oboists into overly fastidious, anal-retentives? Huh!

The Oboe and the English Horn

The word *oboe* is Italian for the French word *hautbois*—h-a-u-t-b-o-i-s—*hautbois*, which means, literally, "high wood." The oboe produces a bright, pungent, nasal tone, and the piercing quality of its sound makes it ideal for tuning the other instruments of the orchestra before a performance. Now, in order to be complete, and to avoid getting myself into any more trouble with my oboist friends than I already have, I'm honor-bound to mention that there is, indeed, an entire oboe family of instruments. That family, from the top down, consists of the oboe, the oboe d'amore (what the Germans call the *Liebesoboe*), the English horn, the baritone oboe, and the heckelphone, or bass oboe. As the oboe d'amore, the baritone oboe, and the heckelphone are rarely used, and are not, therefore, considered standard orchestral instruments, we will, sadly for now, bypass them.

The alto instrument of the double reed family is the English horn, which is pitched roughly five scale steps below the oboe. One of the great mysteries of life, along with the ongoing commercial success of Cheez Whiz and the acting career of Sylvester Stallone, is precisely why the English horn is called the English horn. It is neither of English origin, nor is it a horn. That is, it isn't evolved from an instrument made from an animal's horn. Both the oboe and the English horn evolved from an instrument called a *shawm*, a generic variety of double reed instrument characterized by a reedy and rustic sound, a sound best sampled outdoors. Historically, both the oboe and the English horn have been used to evoke just the sort of earthy, pastoral melancholy associated with their ancestral shawm. As an example of the oboe, the English horn, and the sort of pastoral setting with which they are associated, we turn to the beginning of the third movement of Berlioz' *Symphony fantastique* of 1830, an opening described by Berlioz as consisting of: "Two shepherds piping a shepherd's song in dialogue." The first shepherd is portrayed by the lower English horn; the second by a distant and higher oboe. Let's hear this duet. [**Musical selection:** Hector Berlioz, *Symphonie fantastique* (1830), movement 3, opening]

The Bassoon and the Contrabassoon

A question I've been asked more than once: If there's such a thing as a "bass-oon," shouldn't there also be other members of the "oon" family, like a "sopra-oon" and an "alto-oon?" The answer is no. The bassoon and its ancestors have always been low instruments. Having said that, once upon a time there was a tenor instrument called, yes, yes, yes, a *tenoroon*! However, seeing that no one has actually composed for the tenoroon since the mid-1700s, we can't really consider it as being a viable orchestral instrument. For our information, the word *bassoon* is simply an augmentation of the word *basso*, which is Italian for "bass," as in "a bass double reed."

The bassoon is three instruments in one: dark and heavy in its lower register, clear and sonorous in its middle register, reedy and intense in its upper register, and lyric, penetrating and flexible in all its registers. Among the greatest orchestral examples of the bassoon in its lyric, reedy, and intense upper register is the bassoon solo that begins Igor Stravinsky's *The Rite of Spring* of 1912. [**Musical selection:** Igor Stravinsky, *The Rite of Spring* (1912), opening]

The bassoon is a big instrument. My friends, you need a long tube in order to go down as low as a bassoon can go. So, the instrument is folded back over itself in order to be able to accommodate its length. Now, from a standpoint of sheer size, even more impressive is the contra, or double bassoon, which is folded over itself several times. The contrabassoon is the lowest instrument in the orchestra and its function in the woodwind section is analogous to that of the double basses for the strings, providing the foundation for the entire section. Let's hear the opening of Mozart's Sonata for Bassoon and 'Cello in Bb Major, Köchel 292, played here by two contra-bassoons. Instrumentally, my friends, this is as low as you can go! [**Musical selection:** Wolfgang Mozart, Sonata for Bassoon and 'Cello in Bb Major, 292/K. 196c (1775, arranged for two contrabassoons)] Oh, please! Is the contrabassoon not a fantastic sounding instrument? Oh, I wish I had the nerve to write a piece for piccolo and contrabassoon. Talk about Tweety Pie meets Godzilla!

(A little contrabassoon trivia. There are two different types of contrabassoon: the regular, orchestral model, and the compact opera model. You see, the orchestral model is so darned big that it will actually stick out of the orchestra pit in an opera house and, thus, bobbing around, it would cause a terrific distraction for the audience. So there's also a compact model, the so-called opera-model contra-bassoon, made for use in pit orchestras. I thought you'd like to know!)

The Clarinet Family

Talk about an extended family! The clarinets are the Brady Bunch of the instrumental world. From high-to-low, here are the clarinets that are currently, currently, in use: the sopranino clarinet in Ab, the soprano clarinet in Eb, the clarinet in C, the clarinet in Bb (what we'd consider the standard clarinet), the clarinet in A, the alto clarinet in Eb, the basset horn in F, the bass clarinet in Bb, the contra-alto clarinet in Eb, and the contrabass clarinet in Bb. We might hear all, or nearly all, of those clarinets in a big concert band, or a big marching band, where their mellow, fluid, and homogeneous tone from top-to-bottom makes them an excellent substitute for the strings. However, for the purposes of standard orchestral music (which is the arbitrary limit I've placed on what is already a lengthy exploration of instrumental timbre), for the purposes of standard orchestral music, we need to be aware of three members of the clarinet family: the sopranino clarinet, the standard soprano clarinet in Bb, and the bass clarinet in Bb.

Sidebar—Transposing Instruments

Contrabass clarinet in Bb; basset horn in F; soprano clarinet in Eb: What do these key designations mean? Good question. These key designations indicate that these are transposing instruments, which means that their notated pitches are different from the pitches that actually sound when they play. Now, let's explain by starting at the beginning. Most instruments—keyboards and strings, for example—are what we call non-transposing instruments in concert pitch: When they play a middle C, the pitch that sounds is a middle C. Well, that makes sense, right? A player sees a C written on a page. She plays a C on her instrument and the pitch that sounds is what's called a concert C. But, this is not always the case. For example, when the English horn—which is a transposing instrument, pitched in F—reads that same middle C, the actual pitch that sounds is an F, five steps below that concert C. And here's why.

Show me an English horn player and I'll show you a musician whose original instrument was the oboe. The oboe is a non-transposing instrument pitched in C. When an oboe plays a C, it sounds as a C. Now, in order to make the instruments of the oboe family as easy to play as possible, they all use pretty much the same fingering. Oh, it makes great sense doesn't it? That way, someone trained on the oboe can play any of the instruments of the oboe family—from the English horn to the heckelphone—without having to learn all new fingerings. Except, except, when you finger a C on an English horn, which is longer than an oboe, the actual sound that's produced is going to be five scale-steps lower than the C an oboe would produce with that same fingering. Thus, if a piece of music is in the key of C, and we want the English horn to be in the same key, we need to actually notate its part five steps higher than C—in the key of G—and therefore, when the English horn plays the part written in G, it will sound five steps lower, in the key of concert C! The point: we want to be able to use more or less the same fingerings for all the different trumpets, for all the different clarinets, for all the different saxophones, and so forth. And by using transposing parts, a player of any particular family of instruments need only learn one set of fingerings to be able to play them all.

What this means is that when we look at a score that includes both transposing and non-transposing instruments, we'll see any number of different key signatures, as the transposing instruments will not be notated in the same keys as the non-transposing instruments. Yes, it's confusing. Just be glad, my friends, that you don't have to sit down at a piano and read an orchestral score with four or five different key signatures among the 20 or 25 different instrumental parts. That is as nasty as finding gristle in your cream of wheat.

Back to the Clarinet Family

Clarinet transpositions are based on the soprano clarinet in C, an instrument that, like the oboe, is non-transposing and pitched in concert C. The clarinet in C was used fairly commonly in the 18th and 19th centuries, although it's rarely heard today. The standard clarinet today is the soprano clarinet in Bb, which is slightly longer and has a warmer, rounder tone than the clarinet in C. Let's sample a Bb clarinet. Like all the clarinets, it is a single-reed instrument, employing a wide, thin, spatula-shaped piece of cane fitted against a mouthpiece called a beak. That thin, wide, flexible reed allows clarinetists to make their instrument sing with a nuance and vocality equaled only by the violin and the 'cello. Let's hear the opening of the first movement of Johannes Brahms's ineffably beautiful Quintet for Clarinet and Strings in B Minor of 1891. The clarinet seems virtually to breathe as it sings its part. Please, be aware of the special qualities of the clarinet's three registers, all on display in the following excerpt: the rich warmth of its low, or *chalumeau* register, the round mellowness of its middle register, and the gentle, almost flute-like sweetness of its upper, or *clarino*, register. [**Musical selection:** Johannes Brahms, Quintet for Clarinet and Strings in B Minor, op. 115 (1891), movement 1, opening]

Owing to the width and flexibility of the reed, clarinetists can do the most amazing things with the sound of the clarinet: They can make it growl, bark, bend and, yes, even slide, the most famous example of which being the two-and-one-half-octave upwards slide, or *glissando*, that begins George Gershwin's *Rhapsody in Blue* of 1924. I would tell you how that marvelous glissando came to be. Gershwin composed the *Rhapsody* for a society orchestra led by a bandleader named Paul Whiteman. Gershwin's job was to deliver a piano score, which was to be orchestrated a gentleman named Ferde Grofé. Gershwin wrote the opening as an ascending scale. But, the orchestrator, Ferde Grofé, knew that the clarinetist in the Whiteman band (a guy named Russ Gorman) could play the most amazing glissandi, the likes of which few clarinetists could play at the time. Playing to Gorman's strength, the opening was scored as a clarinet glissando, and now, any clarinetist worth his or her salt can play that glissando that begins the *Rhapsody*.

The sopranino clarinet, while not exactly a commonly heard instrument is, nevertheless, heard often enough that it deserves to be demonstrated here, if only to hear how different its shrill and piercing timbre is from its larger and infinitely more mellow sibling in Bb. Let's hear the famous sopranino clarinet solo from the fifth movement of Hector Berlioz's *Symphonie fantastique*. According to the story of the piece, the sopranino clarinet (and the obscene jig that it plays) represents the former lover of the hero of the piece whom the hero murdered in a drug induced hallucination before the beginning of the fourth movement and who has, here in the fifth movement, returned as a gnarled and evil witch. Don't even ask. Let's hear it. [**Musical selection:** Hector Berlioz, *Symphonie fantastique* (1830), movement 5, sopranino clarinet solo] Talk about the perfect instrument with the perfect instrumental timbre for the expressive job!

My friends, that's the third musical example we've drawn from Berlioz's *Symphonie fantastique* since we began this exploration of timbre, and that begs a little discussion. Should we want to, we could have drawn pretty much every one of our timbral examples from Berlioz's music. He was a fascinating character, an over-the-top Romantic freakazoid, a writer and critic of extraordinary wit and intelligence, and a composer of some of the most outlandish music ever put to paper. Unique among major composers, Berlioz could hardly play any instrument at all. Sure, he could strum a few chords on a guitar, and blow a melody on a flute, but please, by professional standards he was, when it came to playing a musical instrument, nearly illiterate. Except, except when it came to the orchestra! Berlioz played the orchestra the way Liszt played the piano: like a virtuoso. He "heard"—he imagined—music through the medium of the orchestra itself. Berlioz was, very simply, the most original, adventurous, and innovative orchestrator to his time. His use of instruments and instrumental combinations became a model for every generation that followed him, and his treatise on orchestration has been considered a must-read for composers and conductors since its original publication in 1843.

There's one last clarinet to sample before we move on, and that's the fabulous bass clarinet in Bb, an instrument that combines the vocality and agility of a soprano clarinet with the range of a Russian basso singer! Let's hear the opening of the same magnificent Bach Chaconne in D Minor for violin that we heard in Lecture One, arranged here for bass clarinet. [**Musical selection:** Johann Sebastian Bach, Partita no. 2 in D Minor, BWV 1004 (c. 1720), Chaconne, arranged for bass clarinet]

Before we depart the winds we've two more bits of timbre-inspired business: First, an apologia concerning the saxophone family and, second, we must sample that most delicate and refined of all chamber music genres, the wind quintet.

Regarding the saxophones, the saxophone family of instruments was invented by a Belgian named Adolphe Sax for use in 19th-century French military bands. Like the clarinet family, the saxophones employ a single reed. French marching bands notwithstanding, the saxophone family has found its true niche in jazz. Unfortunately, we will not presently investigate the saxophone family of instruments because it's not part of the standard orchestral corps. For this I do apologize.

The Wind Quintet

I trust hearing a little wind quintet music will help to assuage our pain over my cavalier treatment of the saxophone family. What a string quartet is for string players, so a wind quintet is for wind players: the pre-eminent chamber combination involving wind instruments. The standard wind quintet consists of a flute, oboe, clarinet, bassoon, and French horn. Now I know the French horn is a brass instrument and that we haven't yet talked about the brass, but we will, soon enough, and I'd tell you now that the French horn offers an intermediate timbre between the wind and brass choirs, one that reconciles them to each other, meaning that the horn is as timbrally comfortable in the company of wind instruments as it is among brass instruments.

What makes a wind quintet so special for the listener and such a challenge for a composer is its amazing variety of individual instrumental timbres, and the vast number of combinations of timbres those five instruments together can make. In this, the wind quintet is the polar opposite of the string quartet. Where a string quartet is about the blend of homogeneous instruments all drawn from the same instrumental family, a wind quintet is a rainbow of different timbres that somehow must be united into a timbral whole greater than its parts. We turn to Carl Nielsen's magnificent Wind Quintet of 1922. We're going to hear the gorgeous, chorale-like theme that begins the fourth and final movement. [**Musical selection:** Carl Nielsen, Quintet for Winds, op. 43, movement 4, opening]

Dynamics

Ho, ho! I feel another sidebar coming on, one that will take us to the conclusion of this lecture. This sidebar deals with the relative volume—that is, the relative loud and soft in music, something called dynamics. There are two basic categories of dynamics with which we must be conversant: fixed dynamics and graded dynamics. The terminology associated with both categories is Italian, simply because when these terms became standard during the 18th century, Italian was considered the international language of music.

Fixed Dynamics

A fixed dynamic marking is one that indicates a single, unchanging level of volume until another dynamic marking appears to change the first. Fixed dynamics are arrayed around the two polarities of loud and soft, or, properly, *forte* (meaning, literally, in Italian, "strong," "powerful," and "robust"), and *piano* (meaning literally "softly," "quietly," and "gently"). In music notation, *forte* and *piano* are usually indicated, respectively, with an italics letter *f* (meaning *forte*—"loud"), and an italics letter *p* (meaning *piano*—"softly").

Now, my friends, like everything in life, loud and soft, forte and piano, are relative terms. My son Samuel is, at the age of sixteen, about five feet eleven in height. For a member of my family, this makes him huge, but compared to the magnificent Shaquille O'Neal—all seven foot, one inch, 340 pounds of him—my kid's not tall at all. Everything's relative, including the concepts of loud and soft. For example, Beethoven begins his Piano Sonata in C Minor, opus 13, the so-called *Pathétique* sonata, with a fat and juicy C-minor chord, marked *forte*. [**Piano example:** Ludwig van Beethoven, Piano Sonata no. 8 in C Minor, op. 13 (*Pathétique*, 1798), opening] The next event is marked *piano*. [**Piano example:** Ludwig van Beethoven, Piano Sonata no. 8 in C Minor, op. 13 (*Pathétique*, 1798), opening]

Now back to that opening chord. It's clear that Beethoven wants to create a sense of contrast, perhaps even conflict, between the opening chord and the twitching echo that follows it. As such, it's very tempting indeed to want to exaggerate the dynamics, to really whale into that opening chord, and pull way back on the material that follows. [**Piano example:** Ludwig van Beethoven, Piano Sonata no. 8 in C Minor, op. 13 (*Pathétique*, 1798), opening] Then again, from an interpretive point of view, I might be tempted to reduce the dynamic contrast between these two events, and in doing so, create a sense of connection between them. [**Piano example:** Ludwig van Beethoven, Piano Sonata no. 8 in C Minor, op. 13 (*Pathétique*, 1798), opening] Well, which of these versions is correct? I would tell you that they are both correct. Dynamics are relative, and are subject to the interpretive idiosyncrasies of the performer. With the understanding that dynamics are relative, and subject to a degree of interpretive whim, let's fill out the nomenclature. Lying between forte and piano are *mezzo-forte*, which means, literally, "middle, or "sort of loud," and *mezzo-piano*, which means "middle, or "sort of soft.""

(My friends, the Italian *mezzo* means "half" or "middle," and we encounter it constantly. The Italian word for *noon*—*mezzo-giorno*—means, literally, "middle day"; the Italian for midnight—*mezzo-notte*—means, literally, "middle night." A *mezzo soprano* is a female voice midway between a soprano and an alto. In a concert hall, or an opera house, the mezzanine is the intermediate floor between the ground floor and the balcony. And if you're having a day that in English you would call just "so-so," in Italian, you'd say, "*mezzo-mezzo*.")

Back to dynamics! In music notation, mezzo piano is indicated as the letters *mp* in italics, and mezzo forte as *mf* in italics. (Yes, *mf* meant something different when I was growing up, as well, but not here, please, not now!). If we want to indicate that something should be played very loud, we'd notate two italic letter *fs*—*ff*—which is identified with the Italian superlative *fortissimo*. (Adding *issimo* to any Italian word immediately doubles the impact of the word. Hey, try this at home, score some points: "Hey baby, you are, like *ginchissimo*; how about a *kississimo*?" Three *fs*—*fortississimo*—would be *very, very loud*. Four *fs*—*fortiss-iss-issimo*—would be "very, very, very loud," and beyond that, you're wasting your *fs*, unless you want a performer to destroy her instrument trying to play what you've indicated. Likewise, "very quiet"—*pianissimo*—would be notated with two *ps*; "very, very quiet"—*pianississimo*—with three *ps*, and so forth.

Graded Dynamics

Graded dynamics markings are those used to indicate getting progressively louder, or softer. The word *crescendo* means "to get louder"; the words *decrescendo* and *diminuendo* mean "to get softer." For our information, crescendo is the gerund form of the Italian verb *crescere*, which means "to grow," or "increase"; decrescendo and diminuendo are the gerund forms of, respectively "to get smaller" and "to diminish." In musical notation, a crescendo is indicated either by the word itself, the abbreviation *cresc.*, or a what's called an *expanding hairpin*: a small wedge that opens up in the direction of the crescendo. Likewise, a decrescendo, or diminuendo, will be indicated either by the words themselves, the abbreviations *decresc.* or *dim.* or by a "contracting hairpin," a wedge that closes in the direction of the decrescendo. Our vocabulary grows. When we return, we'll conclude our discussion of instrumental timbre with the brass, percussion, and the changing face of the orchestra! Thank you.

Lecture Three
Timbre, Part 3

Scope:
Brass instruments include the French horn, trumpet, trombone, and tuba. Percussion instruments comprise two basic types: pitched and non-pitched. As the orchestra evolved and grew, various instruments were added to the basic string choir of the early 17ᵗʰ-century orchestra. In the 20ᵗʰ century, the complement of percussion instruments used in the orchestra grew substantially.

Outline

I. The English conductor Sir Thomas Beecham once said: "I never look at the brass. It only encourages them." He was referring to the fact that brass instruments, by their very nature, have the power to dominate the orchestra. **Musical selection**: Hector Berlioz, Requiem, op. 5 (1837), *Dies irae/tuba mirum*.

   A. The French horn developed, not in France, but in Germany, and evolved from that most ancient of instruments, a hollowed-out animal horn.

   B. Virtually all modern brass instruments, including the French horn, employ a cup-shaped metal mouthpiece called a *loose-lip mouthpiece*.

   C. The modern horn consists of a gradually tapered, coiled, conical tube of metal around 12 feet in length, with a series of finger-operated valves that vary the overall length of the tubing and, along with the player's lips, thus control the pitch of the instrument.

   D. The French horn is the most difficult brass instrument to play. It takes decades to master the horn's astonishing range of four octaves. **Musical selection**: Richard Strauss, Andante in C Major for Horn and Piano, AV86a (1888).

      1. The French horn occupies the middle ground between the wind and the brass choirs.

      2. In the orchestral music of the Classical Era, the French horns often doubled the strings to reinforce their sound.

      3. The French horn is capable of glorious sound in its own right. **Musical selection**: Robert Schumann, Concert

Piece (*Konzertstück*) for Four French Horns and Orchestra, op. 86 (1849), movement 3.

II. The trumpet has a cylindrical bore that imbues the instrument with a much brighter and more piercing sound than the horn.

    A. Like the clarinet, the trumpet belongs to an extended family of instruments:

        1. Piccolo trumpet

        2. Bass trumpet in Bb

        3. Cornet in Bb

        4. Cornet in Eb

        5. Flugelhorn in Bb

        6. "Standard" trumpet in Bb

        7. "Standard" trumpet in C

    B. In the following excerpt, we should be aware of the agility of the solo trumpet and the incredibly fast repeated notes that can be played using double-tonguing technique. **Musical selection**: Georg Philipp Telemann, Concerto in F Minor for Oboe, Strings, and Continuo, TWV 51:e1 (1712–1721), arranged for trumpet, movement 3.

III. The low brass consists of the trombone and the tuba.

    A. As an example of low brass sound, we hear the following excerpt in which the three trombones imbue the music with magisterial dignity. **Musical selection**: Robert Schumann, Symphony no. 3 in Eb Major, op. 97 (*Rhenish*, 1850), movement 4, opening.

    B. The trombone is the most primitive of any modern instrument. The basic trombone has no valves, no keys, no levers, and no pads, just a slide by which the player manually extends or shortens the overall length of the instrument.

        1. The simplicity of the trombone's design produces one of the purest sounds on the planet.

        2. The slide makes it the most vocally flexible brass instrument. In terms of its lyric capabilities, the trombone is equal to the clarinet and the violin.

        3. The trombone family consists of seven different instruments, of which we generally hear only two in a modern orchestra: the tenor trombone and the bass trombone.

    4. Most modern orchestras feature two tenor trombones, one bass trombone, and a tuba to round out the low end of the brass.

C. The name *tuba* has been applied to many instruments over the years, including the euphonium, baritone, tenor horn, helicon, sousaphone, and Wagner tuba. What they all have in common is that they consist of a long, conical bore and are operated using valves.

    1. What we call *tubas* today—the bass and contrabass saxhorns—anchor the brass choir in the same way that the double basses anchor the string choir and the contrabassoon anchors the wind choir.

    2. Saxhorns are surprisingly agile, despite their size, and have a fantastically deep range. **Musical selection**: Gustav Mahler, Symphony no. 1 in D Major (*Titan*, 1888), movement 3, tuba (saxhorn) entry.

IV. The brass quintet is the preeminent chamber combination involving brass instruments.

A. The standard brass quintet consists of two trumpets, French horn, tenor trombone, and bass trombone or two trumpets, French horn, tenor trombone, and tuba.

B. The individual instruments of a brass quintet blend into a homogeneous whole, with the French horn acting as the "timbral glue," connecting the trumpets with the low brass.

C. Modern brass instruments are about power and brilliance, as exemplified in the following musical excerpt. **Musical selection**: Samuel Scheidt, *Galliard battaglia* (c. 1621).

V. There are two basic categories of percussion instruments: pitched and non-pitched. A pitched percussion instrument produces a clear fundamental pitch, a sound that can be sung. A non-pitched percussion instrument produces a sound that cannot be sung.

A. Pitched percussion instruments include the timpani, mallet instruments (such as the orchestral bells, or glockenspiel, xylophone, vibraphone, and marimba), celesta, and tubular bells.

B. Non-pitched percussion instruments include drums, triangle, cymbals, and the orchestral gong (tam-tam).

C. The timpani (kettle drums), which require a specialist to play (a timpanist), come in a variety of sizes and are typically played in groups of three or four.

1. Each *tympanum* (singular of timpani) is capable of playing the distance of a fifth (five white keys on the piano).

2. By using an array of three or four different-sized drums, a considerable range of pitches becomes available.

3. Modern timpani are built with a foot pedal that tightens and loosens the drumhead, allowing the instrument to be retuned during the course of a performance.

4. At any given moment, each tympanum is tuned to a single pitch, so that the timpanist can play three or four particular pitches. During the course of a performance, the timpanist must constantly retune each tympanum by putting his ear just above the drumhead and tapping it with his finger, while moving the pedal with his foot until the pitch is correct.

5. Retuning during the course of a performance requires a great deal of skill. The timpanist may have only a few seconds to retune all of his timpani, and he does this while the timpani themselves vibrate sympathetically with the music being played by the rest of the orchestra.

6. Beethoven was the first composer to treat the timpani, collectively, as a genuine and independent instrument. **Musical selection**: Ludwig van Beethoven, Symphony no. 9 in D Minor, op. 125 (1824), movement 2, opening.

D. It takes training and skill to develop the fine sense of timing that is required in the percussion section. Every instrument, even the tiny triangle, can be clearly heard among the other orchestral instruments. **Musical selection**: Johannes Brahms, Symphony no. 4 in E Minor, op. 98 (1885), movement 3, opening.

VI. The orchestra came into existence as a result of the 17th-century opera house.

A. By the end of the 17th century, the core of orchestral strings had been joined, in the larger and wealthier opera houses, by flutes, oboes, bassoons, trumpets, and even, on occasion, trombones.

B. By the 1740s, the great composers of the High Baroque (Johann Sebastian Bach, George Frederick Handel, Georg Philipp Telemann, and Antonio Vivaldi) had created a body of magnificent orchestral music that remains an essential part of the orchestral repertoire to this day.

C. The High Baroque orchestra was of two generic types:

1. The basic group consisted entirely of strings—plus the ubiquitous harpsichord accompaniment (*continuo*)—numbering between 12 and 16 players. **Musical selection**: Antonio Vivaldi, Violin Concerto in E Major, op. 8, no. 1 ("Spring" from *The Four Seasons*, c. 1725).

2. The second type of Baroque orchestra is the *festive* orchestra: a string orchestra with any number of wind and/or brass and percussion instruments added to the mix. Outside the opera house, such orchestras were usually pick-up groups put together for a special occasion. **Musical selection**: George Frederick Handel, *Music for the Royal Fireworks* (1749), overture, conclusion.

D. In the 18th century, with the rise of the symphony as a compositional genre and the growing popularity of the orchestra as a performance medium among the aristocracy and the middle class, the orchestra continued to expand.

1. Horns became a standard orchestral instrument, and by the turn of the 19th century, the clarinet was as well. The strings were still the backbone of the orchestra, and winds and brass were most often employed to support and reinforce the string sound, rather than as important instrumental timbres in their own right. **Musical selection**: Joseph Haydn, Symphony no. 94 in G Major (*Surprise*, 1791), movement 4, opening.

2. In explicitly celebratory orchestral works, trumpets and drums were added to create a pomp-filled environment. **Musical selection**: Wolfgang Mozart, Symphony no. 34 in C Major, K. 338 (1780), movement 1, opening.

3. Mozart had a particular affinity for the wind choir, which he featured in his orchestral music to a degree most unusual in his day. **Musical selection**: Wolfgang Mozart, Symphony in G Minor, K. 550 (1788), movement 3, trio.

E. By the 1830s, the public concert had replaced the private, aristocratic entertainment as the essential orchestral venue.

    1. Large standing orchestras performing in public concert halls became the orchestral norm.

    2. The growing orchestra reflected a basic Romantic-Era article of faith that bigger was better in terms of musical expression. Berlioz wrote that his ideal orchestra consisted of 467 players: 242 strings, 30 harps, 30 pianos, 12 cymbals, 16 French horns, and a wide variety of percussion!

    3. Gustav Mahler's Symphony no. 8 came to be known as the *Symphony of a Thousand* because of the number of performers, orchestral and vocal, who were reported to have participated in the premiere. **Musical selection**: Gustav Mahler, Symphony no. 8 in Eb Major (1906), finale, part 2.

F. Perhaps the biggest single change in the 20th-century orchestra was the demand by composers for an entirely new number and variety of percussion instruments. **Musical selection**: Igor Stravinsky, *The Rite of Spring* (1912), "Sacrificial Dance."

Lecture Three—Transcript
Timbre, Part 3

This is Lecture Three and it is entitled "Timbre, Part 3." Among the very many great lines uttered by the English conductor Sir Thomas Beecham is: "I never look at the brass. It only encourages them." What ever would have caused Sir Thomas to say such a thing? Well, I'll show you. Let's hear a portion of the *Dies irae* from Hector Berlioz's Requiem, opus 5 of 1837. [**Musical selection:** Hector Berlioz, Requiem, op. 5 (1837), *Dies irae/Tuba mirum*] Magnificent! When a full brass choir begins to wail, there's pretty much no sound on the planet that's more powerful, more magisterial, more viscerally moving.

But, back to Thomas Beecham's comment. The orchestral composer, wanting a bit of climactic punch in a given section of music, might indicate a dynamic of fortissimo: loud, yes, but certainly not enough to induce a nosebleed. Your average orchestra will have around 60 strings, 12 winds, and 10 brass. Now, I would tell you that for most brass players, a dynamic of piano is beneath contempt, mezzo-piano is an insult, mezzo-forte is uncomfortably limiting, forte is permission, and fortissimo, well, fortissimo is probably a mistake. Why? Because the brass may be outnumbered 72 to 10 in a modern orchestra, but they are certainly not outgunned and they will bury, they will absolutely bury, the rest of the orchestra (except the piccolo), if they are given even half a chance to do so. So, conductors spend much of their professional lives attempting to quiet the brass, attempting to reign in the brass, attempting to balance the brass with the rest of the orchestra. Like herding cats, it's a dirty, difficult, often impossible task. The brass players themselves—particularly the trumpet, trombone, and tuba players, almost all of whom grew up playing in marching bands—chose their instruments just because they could wail, just because they were shiny and loud and macho. Asking a brass choir to play pianissimo is like asking a Ferrari to stay under the speed limit; it goes against the very grain of what the instruments are all about. "I never look at the brass. It only encourages them." Wise words from a great conductor.

The French Horn

Like the English horn, the designation *French horn* is another case of an instrument whose name has nothing to do with its country of origin. The French horn was, in reality, developed in what is today Germany. Like any instrument correctly called a horn, the French horn evolved from that most ancient of instruments, a hollowed out animal horn, "Bronx-cheered into" at the narrow end. What is a Bronx-cheer my friends, but the lips of the player vibrating together just like a double reed! Virtually all modern brass instruments—the French horn included—use a cup-shaped metal mouthpiece that is called a loose-lip mouthpiece. The modern French horn, or simply horn, consists of a gradually tapered conical tube of metal around 12 feet in length, coiled for your convenience and portability, with a series of finger-operated valves that vary the overall length of the tubing and therefore, along with the player's lips, control the pitch of the instrument. The French horn is the most difficult instrument to play in the orchestra. Just to initiate a sound without smearing, or fluffing, takes years of work and it takes decades to master the horn's full range: an astonishing four octaves, from an F two and a half octaves below middle C to an F an octave and a half above middle C. Some horn music! The opening of Richard Strauss's Andante for Horn and Piano in C Major of 1888. [**Musical selection:** Richard Strauss, Andante for Horn and Piano in C Major, AV 86a (1888)]

As we discussed in Lecture Two apropos of the wind quintet, the French horn occupies a sort of middle ground between the wind and the brass choirs. Its conical tube produces a gorgeously round and mellow tone, one that blends equally well with the winds, strings, and brass. In the orchestral music of the Classical Era, for example, as often as not the horns doubled (that is, played the same notes as) the strings, in order to reinforce and give body and depth to the string sound. Of course, the horns make a glorious noise when put front and center and, for that, we turn to the conclusion of the third and final movement of Robert Schumann's *Konzertstück* ("Concert Piece") for four French Horns and Orchestra of 1849. [**Musical selection:** Robert Schumann, Concert Piece for Four French Horns and Orchestra, op. 86 (1849), movement 3] Sensational!

The Trumpet

Unlike the horn, whose tube is conical (that is, it flares outwards), a substantial portion of the tube, or bore, of a trumpet is cylindrical, something that imbues the instrument with a much brighter and more piercing timbre than the horn. Like the clarinet, the trumpets comprise an extended instrumental family, consisting of seven trumpets: the piccolo trumpet and the bass trumpet in Bb; the cornets in Bb and Eb; the flugelhorn in Bb; and the standard trumpets in Bb and C. The standard trumpets in Bb and C, which together are the soprano voice of the brass section, are almost exactly the same size. The Bb is the more common instrument; the C the slightly more brilliant. Bb or C trumpet? Well, it's usually left up to individual performer to decide which instrument to play. Let's hear some lovely trumpet playing: the third movement of Georg Philipp Telemann's Concerto in F Minor for Oboe, arranged for a modern trumpet. My friends, let's glory in the agility and brilliance of the solo trumpet, and let's be especially aware of the incredibly fast repeated notes the trumpet plays, using a technique called double tonguing. Try that on a French horn, and you'll need an oral surgeon to get your tongue out of the instrument! [**Musical selection;** Georg Philipp Telemann, Concerto in F Minor for Oboe, Strings, and Continuo, TWV 51:e1 (1712–21), arranged for trumpet, movement 3]

The Low Brass

Low brass: two words guaranteed to fill other musicians with fear and loathing! As a group, low brass players can be a pretty wild bunch, with their big horns and big spit valves and their Homer Simpson beer bottle openers dangling from their belts. Having said that, no one can question the majesty, gravity and dignity of the sound that they together can create! As an example of the low brass sound, let's hear the opening of the fourth movement of Robert Schumann's Symphony no. 3 of 1850. Subtitled the *Rhenish* or the *Rhineland* Symphony, this movement was inspired by a ceremony Schumann witnessed at the awesome Cathedral of Cologne in September of 1850. Schumann indicates that the movement be played "in the character of an accompaniment to a solemn processional." While we listen, let's focus on the magisterial dignity of this music, a function of the three trombones in the bass. [**Musical** selection: Robert Schumann, Symphony no. 3 in Eb Major, op. 97 (*Rhenish*, 1850), movement 4, opening]

The Trombone

From a purely technological point of view, the trombone is the most "primitive" of any modern instrument: plumbing with a mouthpiece. Your basic trombone has no valves, no keys, no levers, no stuff. Instead, it's got a slide, by which the player manually extends, or shortens, the overall length of the instrument. Your basic tenor trombone is nine feet long with the slide fully retracted (that's in what's called first position), and about 14 feet long with the slide fully extended (in what's called seventh position). A trombone is the only modern orchestral instrument that you can build in your garage with about $20 worth of PVC piping. Like I said, plumbing. And yet! Having blindsided the trombone for its technological simplicity, we're going to turn around and suggest that its simplicity is a virtue, and not a flaw! My friends, if the shortest distance between any two points is a straight line; if less truly is more; if the fewer bells and whistles you put between the source and the sound creates a less corrupted, less distorted sound, then the trombone is the personification of just enough! The simplicity of its design belies a great truth: the trombone produces one of the purest, least distorted sounds on the planet and, because of the nuances in pitch made possible by the slide, it is by far the most vocally flexible brass instrument. In terms of its lyric capabilities, the trombone is the equal to the clarinet, violin, and the 'cello. While the trombone family consists of seven different instruments, we will generally hear only two trombones in a modern orchestra: the tenor trombone, and the bass trombone. Most modern orchestras will feature two tenor trombones and one bass trombone, with a tuba rounding out the low end of the brass.

The Tuba

The word *tuba* is an odd-sounding and frankly confusing designation: it's been applied to so many different instruments over the years as to become more a generic label than an actual instrument. A modern orchestral tuba is, in reality, an instrument called a bass, or contrabass saxhorn. Other instruments that have been called tubas include the euphonium, the baritone, the tenor horn, the helicon, the sousaphone, and the so-called Wagner tubas, an instrument devised by Richard Wagner for use in his epic cycle of music dramas, *The Ring of the Niebelung*. What all these diverse instruments have in common is that they consist of a long, conical bore, or tube and are operated using valves. What we understand as tubas today—the bass and contrabass saxhorns—anchor the brass choir in the same way the double basses anchor the string choir and the contrabassoon anchors the wind choir. Despite their size and fantastically deep range, the saxhorns are surprisingly agile instruments. It's a stock-in-trade given that a junior, or senior-year, conservatory tuba recital will include a tuba transcription of Rimsky Korsakov's *The Flight of the Bumblebee*, an experience we will, mercifully, forego for now. Instead, we return to the bizarre, funeral-march version of *Frère Jacques* that opens the third movement of Mahler's Symphony no. 1. We first sampled the movement in order to hear the solo double bass that actually begins the movement, but if we listen just a little further, we'll hear the tuba play its own version of the tune. [**Musical selection:** Gustav Mahler, Symphony no. 1 in D Major (*Titan*, 1888), movement three, tuba entry]

Brass Quintet

A brass quintet is for brass players what a string quartet is for string players and a wind quintet is for wind players: the pre-eminent chamber combination involving brass instruments. The standard brass quintet consists of two trumpets, a French horn, a tenor trombone and a bass trombone, or two trumpets, a French horn, a tenor trombone and a tuba. Like a string quartet and unlike a woodwind quintet, the individual instrumental timbres of a brass quintet blend into a homogeneous whole, with the French horn acting as the timbral glue that connects the trumpets with the low brass. Modern brass instruments are about power and brilliance, both of which are in high relief in the following arrangement for brass quintet of a galliard (a galliard is a type of Renaissance dance) composed by the German Samuel Scheidt around 1621. For our information: the quintet on our recording employs a bass trombone, rather than a tuba. [**Musical selection**: Samuel Scheidt, *Galliard battaglia* (c. 1621)]

The Percussion

Categories and distinctions! Categories first! There are two basic categories of percussion instruments: pitched and non-pitched percussion instruments. A pitched percussion instrument is one that produces a clear fundamental pitch that we can sing along with. A non-pitched, or noise instrument, is one that produces a sound we cannot sing along with. We'll discuss the nature of noise in Lecture Seven. For now, let's identify the instruments themselves.

Pitched percussion instruments include the timpani; the mallet instruments (meaning those instruments played with rubber, wood, or yarn-headed mallets: the orchestral bells, also known as a glockenspiel; the xylophone; the vibraphone; and the marimba); the celesta (which is a glockenspiel operated by a piano-like keyboard, rather than one manually struck with mallets); and the tubular bells (also known as orchestral chimes), which sound very much like the chimes in a grandfather clock.

Non-pitched percussion instruments include the drums, triangle, cymbals, and the orchestral gong, which is properly called a *tam-tam*. And, my friends, I'll tell you why it is properly called a tam-tam! A gong is a pitched percussion instrument of Chinese origin, which is only rarely used in Western orchestral music. A tam-tam, which is essentially a huge cymbal, is a non-pitched percussion instrument of Turkish origin, and it is commonly used in Western orchestral music. What is often called an orchestral gong should, properly, be called a tam-tam. You needed to know that.

Categories and distinctions! We've observed the two main categories of percussion instruments: pitched and non-pitched. Now an essential distinction. Percussionists—not drummers; don't call them drummers—percussionists play all the percussion instruments except one and that would be the timpani, or the kettle-drums. An orchestra might boast, oh, four or five percussionists, most of whom could, if they had to, fill in on the timpani. But, in reality, the timpani are incredibly difficult to play, and they require a specialist. They require a *timpanist*. You would no more want to call a timpanist a percussionist, or worse, a drummer, than you'd want to call an

Irishman an Englishman, or a New Zealander an Australian. Them's fightin' words, and timpanists own mallets and they know how to wield them!

Timpani come in a variety of sizes, and are typically played in groups of three or four. Each *timpanum* (the singular of timpani) is capable of playing the range of a fifth—five white keys on a piano—so that by using an array of three or four different sized drums, a not-inconsiderable range of pitches becomes available. Modern timpani are built with a foot pedal that tightens and loosens the drumhead and thus allows a timpanist to constantly retune the instrument during the course of a performance. And thus, the great challenge of playing the timpani, above and beyond mere stick technique. My friends, a timpanist is typically surrounded by four timpani of different sizes. At any given moment, each timpanum is tuned to a single pitch, so at any given moment, the timpanist can play four particular pitches. But, composers are constantly asking the timpanist to play different pitches. And so, during the course of a performance, a timpanist must constantly retune each timpanum by putting his ear just above the drumhead and tapping it with his finger while moving the pedal with his foot until the pitch is correct. All of this must be done while the orchestra is playing and as the timpani themselves vibrate sympathetically with the music being played. There are times when a timpanist might have only 30 or 40 seconds to retune all four timpani, pick up his mallets, and be ready to go. A timpanist must have the ears of a bat, nerves of steel, and be able to count like an atomic clock. Hey, if a violinist misses an entrance, who's going to know? But, if the timpanist misses an entrance, it's as obvious as a centipede on Mona Lisa's nose.

Beethoven was the first composer to treat the timpani, collectively, as a genuine and independent instrument. As an example, we turn to the opening of the second movement of Beethoven's Symphony no. 9 of 1824, a movement that begins by actually treating the timpani as a solo instrument! [**Musical selection:** Ludwig van Beethoven, Symphony no. 9 in D Minor, op. 125 (1824), movement 2, opening] Never call a timpanist a drummer. And never, ever say anything bad about Beethoven in front of a timpanist. My friends, just don't.

Sidebar—Are the Percussionists Paid the Same Amount of Money as Other Members of the Orchestra?

Okay, we go to an orchestral concert, and Johannes Brahms's Symphony no. 4 of 1885 is on the program. The joyful, buoyant third movement begins, and about 37 seconds into the movement we are greeted by the bright, metallic ringing of a triangle. [**Musical selection:** Johannes Brahms, Symphony no. 4 in E Minor, op. 98 (1885), movement 3, opening] Having watched the percussionist play that triangle, some of us might very well think: "I wonder if they pay that percussionist the same amount as they do the string players. Jeez, I could of done that." Well, no, you couldn't. For a percussionist, there's a lifetime of training behind her ability to strike and strike with confidence and conviction at exactly the right moment, not a millisecond too soon or too late. My friends, if orchestral musicians were paid by the note, the violinists would all be millionaires. But, musicians are not paid by the note; they're paid for their expertise and, in the case of percussionists, their ability to negotiate risk. As we observed apropos of the timpani, in most sections of the orchestra there is a degree of anonymity that percussion players—who are standing up and playing loud instruments one at a time—do not have.

To answer the question: Yes, a full-time professional percussionist makes as much money as any full-time member of the orchestra. And the timpanist makes as much as any section leader, except the first first-violinist, the *concert master*, who is usually the highest paid musician in the orchestra. Sidebar over.

The Orchestra

The orchestra, as we understand it today—a fixed body of instruments for which a composer specifically composes—is a product of the 17th-century opera house. The growing expressive demands of the opera house put ever-greater demands on the instrumental ensembles, or orchestras that accompanied early opera. By the end of the 17th century, the core of orchestral strings had been joined, in the larger and wealthier opera houses, by flutes, oboes, bassoons, trumpets, and even, on occasion, trombones. It was at just this time—the 1680s and 1690s—that orchestral music, primarily in the form of concerti, began being composed for its own sake. By the 1740s, the great composers of the High, or Late Baroque—Johann Sebastian Bach, George Frederick Handel, Georg Philipp Telemann, and Antonio Vivaldi—had created a body of magnificent orchestral music that remains an essential part of the orchestral repertoire to this day.

The Baroque Orchestra

The High Baroque orchestra came in two generic types. The most common type was what's called today the basic, or standard, Baroque orchestra: a group consisting entirely of strings, plus the ubiquitous harpsichord accompaniment, an orchestra numbering anywhere between 12 and 16 players. In his four violin concerti collectively known as *The Seasons*, Antonio Vivaldi employed just such a "standard" orchestra. As an example, let's hear the opening of the first concerto of the set, the ubiquitous, but by no means unworthy, Violin Concerto in E Major, op. 8, no. 1, subtitled "Spring." Here we go, your basic High Baroque string orchestra, consisting here of a total of 16 performers. [**Musical selection:** Antonio Vivaldi, Violin Concerto in E Major, op. 8, no. 1 ("Spring," c. 1725)]

The second generic type of Baroque orchestra is the so-called festive orchestra: a string orchestra with any number of wind and/or brass and percussion instruments added to the mix. Outside of the opera house, such orchestras were usually pick-up groups, put together for some special occasion. For example, George Frederick Handel's in-all-ways awesome *Music for the Royal Fireworks* of 1749 was composed for an orchestra consisting of 41 players, small by modern standards, but, for its time, gigantic and magnificent, as befit its dedicatee, the English king, George II, for whom the piece was composed! We hear the conclusion of the overture. Handel, *Music for the Royal Fireworks*, 1749. [**Musical selection:** George Frederick Handel, *Music for the Royal Fireworks* (1749), overture, conclusion]

The Classical-Era Orchestra

With the rise of the symphony as a compositional genre and the growing popularity of the orchestra as a performance medium among both the aristocracy and the growing middle class, the orchestra continued to expand. The string corps was enlarged, now including the newly developed double bass. Horns became a standard orchestral instrument and, by the turn of the 19th century, the clarinet as well. Having said that, the strings were still the backbone of the orchestra, and winds and brass were most often employed to support and reinforce the string sound, rather than as important instrumental timbres on their own. Let's hear, as an example, the fourth movement of Haydn's Symphony no. 94 of 1791. [**Musical selection:** Joseph Haydn, Symphony no. 94 in G Major (*Surprise*, 1791), movement 4, opening] In explicitly celebratory orchestral works, trumpets and drums were added to create an appropriately pomp-filled timbral environment, as in the first movement opening of Mozart's Symphony no. 34 of 1780. [**Musical selection:** Wolfgang Mozart, Symphony no. 34 in C Major, K. 338 (1780), movement 1, opening] Mozart had a particular affinity for the wind choir, which he featured in his orchestral music to a degree most unusual for his day. For example, during the middle section of the third movement of his Symphony in G Minor of 1788, Mozart absolutely wallows in the sounds of the horns and winds. The result is an exquisite passage that offers a wonderful contrast with the string-dominated music that surrounds it. Let's hear that wind- and horn-dominated passage. [**Musical selection:** Wolfgang Mozart, Symphony in G Minor, K. 550 (1788), movement 3, trio]

The Romantic Orchestra

The 19th century administered a major dose of growth hormone to the orchestra. By the 1830s, the public concert had replaced the private, aristocratic entertainment as the essential orchestral venue. It was during the 19th century that large standing orchestras performing in large public concert halls became the orchestral norm, a norm which continues to this day. The growing orchestra reflected a basic Romantic-Era article of faith: that when it came to musical expression, bigger was better. In fact, in the post-Beethoven, self-expression-at-all-costs world of the 19th century, big was not only better, it became an essential aesthetic element unto itself: big orchestras could create just that sort of power, awe, and amazement that were the essence of Romantic art, transporting the audience away from the every day to a place quite beyond anything they had experienced before. Hector Berlioz's *Symphonie fantastique* was a product of just this sort of over-the-top expressive impulse, one that saw the orchestra balloon upwards from the 25–35 piece ensembles of the late 18th century to the often 100-plus-piece ensembles of the 19th century. For our information, Berlioz wrote that his ideal orchestra consisted of 467 players—an ensemble that included 242 strings, 30 harps, 30 pianos, 12 cymbals, 16 French horns, and a wide variety of percussion. As Harold Schonberg points out: "No wonder his friends considered him impractical and his enemies crazy." (Schonberg, 3rd edition, 157.) Well, no crazier than Gustav Mahler, whose own Symphony no. 8 came to be known as the *Symphony of a Thousand* because of the number of performers, orchestral and vocal, who were reported to have participated in its premiere. We hear the grandiloquent final minutes of this Symphony no. 8. [**Musical selection:** Gustav Mahler, Symphony no. 8 in Eb Major (1906), part 2, finale]

The 20th-Century Orchestra

Perhaps the biggest single change in the 20th-century orchestra was the demand by composers for an entirely new number and variety of percussion instruments. Now, this should come as no surprise. As Western composers became ever more aware of non-Western musics, so the explosive, driving, and even violent sensibility of those non-Western musics became a basic syntactical element of 20th-century concert music. An early 20th-century example of this is Igor Stravinsky's *The Rite of Spring*, a piece of music meant to evoke the mating rituals and human sacrifice of Bronze-Age Russia. What better way to create the ancient, brutal, powerful, and ritualistic musical sensibility the ballet called for than with a huge percussion battery? We hear the conclusion of the "Sacrificial Dance" that itself ends *The Rite of Spring*. [**Musical selection:** Igor Stravinsky, *The Rite of Spring* (1912), "Sacrificial Dance"]

Conclusion

Clearly, this investigation of timbre could go on forever. But, we've new musical fields to plow. Perhaps the best thing we can do by way of a homework assignment is to make ourselves aware—consciously aware—of the timbre of whatever music we might by chance be listening to. This is especially true when listening to mixed ensembles like an orchestra, where, if we're not listening carefully, we tend to hear the sound of the ensemble like a puree of its constituent instrumental parts, rather than as a rich and varied composite of its individual instrumental parts. My friends, to the degree that we can, let's be aware of the instrumental combinations that together create the sound, the timbre of the music we listen to. Let us pause to revel in the sound of the music for its own sake, as a feast for the ears! In doing so, we'll hear the voice with which a composer is communicating his, or her ideas directly to us! Thank you.

Lecture Four
Beat and Tempo

Scope:
Having explored some of the timbral (sound) aspects of music, we now move on to the time aspect of music (rhythm). The *beat*, which is the shortest time division to which we can comfortably move our bodies, can transmit a great deal of musical and expressive information. The speed of the beat—the *tempo*—can be designated by a musical linguistic term, which is subject to individual interpretation, or it can be specified by a precise metronome marking. A beat can be steady and even, or it can be imprecise and sometimes even imperceptible.

Outline

I. We have explored the most easily perceived facets of the sound aspect of music, as in our definition of music as "sound in time." We now move on to explore the time aspects of music.

   A. *Time* in music means "rhythm," but the word *rhythm* is too general a term to be useful. We will use more specific vocabulary.

   B. The shortest time division to which we can comfortably move our bodies is called the *beat*, or *pulse*. **Musical selection**: John Philip Sousa, *The Stars and Stripes Forever* (1896).

   1. "To which we can comfortably move our bodies" is a subjective definition of *beat*. **Musical selection**: John Philip Sousa, *The Stars and Stripes Forever* (repeated at different speeds, or *tempi*).

   2. Powerful beats affect us metabolically. The power of movement or dance is instinctive.

   3. Once the beat is established, it becomes the continuum on which the entire musical structure rests until the composer or performer chooses to alter that beat and, thus, create a new continuum.

   4. It is amazing how much musical and expressive information is transmitted via the beat in a given section of music: the beat's relative strength, its speed, how certain beats are emphasized or accented, and how beats are grouped or not grouped. The beat in the Sousa excerpt is grouped in sets of two (or four). **Musical selection**: John Philip Sousa, *The Stars and Stripes Forever* (1896).

5. The following musical excerpt is an example of beats that are grouped in threes. **Musical selection**: Johannes Brahms, Waltzes for Piano Four Hands, op. 39, no. 4 (1865). (This excerpt is repeated.) The beat in this piece tells us that this is a dance, and its grouping in threes tells us that it is a three-step dance called a waltz.

C. The relative speed of a passage of music is its *tempo*. There are six basic tempo designations. (These, like other musical terms, are traditionally in Italian.)

1. *Presto*: very fast
2. *Allegro*: fast
3. *Andante*: moderate, or walking speed
4. *Adagio*: moderately slow
5. *Lento*: slow
6. *Largo*: very slow

D. Those tempo designations are subject to individual interpretation. **Piano examples**: Wolfgang Mozart, Piano Sonata in C Major, K. 545 (1788), movement 1, opening (played at three different speeds, or tempi).

E. In 1815, a Viennese builder of mechanical musical instruments named Johann Nepomuk Maelzel patented the metronome.

1. This device can be set to produce a clicking sound from 40 to 200 times a minute, thereby allowing a composer to designate a precise means of establishing the tempo. **Piano example**: Wolfgang Mozart, Piano Sonata in C Major, K. 545 (1788), movement 1, opening (played at 116 beats per minute).

2. Not all conductors choose to honor a composer's metronome marking. The opening of Beethoven's third symphony, which is marked at 60 beats per minute, has been recorded at a slower tempo. **Piano example**: Ludwig van Beethoven Symphony no. 3 in Eb Major, op. 55 (*Eroica*, 1803), movement 1, opening (played at

60 beats a minute). **Musical selections**: Ludwig van Beethoven, Symphony no. 3 in Eb Major, op. 55 (*Eroica*, 1803), movement 1, opening (played at 46 beats per minute and at 60 beats per minute).

II. The last 30 years have seen a revival of period instruments in recordings. The relative merits of period instruments versus modern instruments have been hotly debated.

    A. To argue that we should hear Beethoven's music the way his audiences heard it assumes that there was a fixed instrumental standard in Beethoven's time. There was not. In his own day, Beethoven would have been unlikely to have heard as high a quality of performance as has been achieved in modern performances of his music.

    B. The real issue here centers on what the composer indicates in terms of balance, articulation, and tempo.

        1. Beethoven scored his Symphony no. 3 for two flutes, two oboes, two clarinets, two bassoons, three French horns, two trumpets, timpani, and strings.

        2. The string section would have numbered about 40 instruments, playing on gut rather than steel strings, resulting in an overall orchestral complement of 54 players. **Musical selection**: Ludwig van Beethoven, Symphony no. 3 in Eb Major, op. 55 (1803), movement 1, opening.

        3. In that recording, the conductor respected the size of the string choir that Beethoven would most likely have used, retaining a crisp and beautiful balance. A larger, modern string choir would have drowned out the winds and brass.

    C. In the 19th century, the strings were modified to make them capable of playing louder but at the cost of flexibility. It is easier to player faster on period stringed instruments, and therefore, it is easier to honor the sorts of faster tempos and articulations that were created with these instruments in mind.

III. A beat may not be steady and even. It may not even be perceivable.

    A. **Musical selection**: Harry von Tilzer and Joseph Lamb, *A*

Bird in a Gilded Cage (1900). Here, the beat speeds up and slows down with the natural rhetorical ebb and flow of the storytelling.

B. In that recording of *A Bird in a Gilded Cage*, the performance took a very flexible approach to beat. It speeded up the beat (*accelerando*) and slowed down the beat (*ritardando*) constantly.

    1. The term for this flexibility of beat is *rubato* ("robbed time").

    2. The Polish-born composer and pianist Frédéric Chopin was famous for his rubato. **Piano examples**: Frédéric Chopin, Mazurka in A Minor, op. 17, no. 4 (played as a dance and played as a song of regret).

C. The absence of an easily perceived beat often creates tension.

    1. Richard Wagner's music drama *Tristan und Isolde* illustrates the use of orchestral rubato to produce a sense of unease.

    2. The story of *Tristan und Isolde* concerns two lovers who cannot consummate their physical passion. By denying any semblance of beat for the first two minutes of the overture to this music drama, Wagner conveys that sense of frustration. **Musical selection**: Richard Wagner, *Tristan und Isolde* (1859), overture, opening.

    3. This is a case in which notation and perception are two very different things. Although the notated music looks normal, the score indicates that the music should be played *lento* (very slowly) and with long pauses (*fermatas*).

    4. More than following the notated rhythms in their parts, the players are following the conductor's baton. Time is so stretched by this orchestral rubato that a regular beat is hardly perceived at all.

Lecture Four—Transcript
Beat and Tempo

This is Lecture Four. It is entitled "Beat and Tempo." My friends, back in Lecture One, we defined music as simply as we could, as being sound in time, or as time defined by sound. To this point of the course, we have discussed those most accessible and easily perceived facets of the sound aspect of music: instrumental timbre and dynamics. It's now time to begin an exploration of the time aspect of music. When we talk about the time aspect of music, we're talking about some aspect of rhythm.

We contemplate the word rhythm. Aside from being at the extremely short end of the "vowel stick" the word is, frankly, almost too general to be of any use. We can talk endlessly about harmonic rhythm, body rhythm, innate rhythm, the rhythm of the spheres, the rhythm method, "I got rhythm, who could ask for anything more?" and so forth. So, aside from occasional use, we will do our best to avoid the word rhythm entirely, in favor of more specific terminology. Terminology. Oh, I wish it wasn't as important as it is, but it is. I'm a firm believer that if we have words with which we can identify non-verbal phenomena—like a musical event, or the taste of a wine, or the smell of a flower—we will be able to recognize and distinguish those phenomena to a degree and with a confidence far beyond that which we would, if we didn't have the verbal means to identify them. Look, we all laugh at wine talk, but it works. Without a vocabulary with which to identify the subtleties of taste, texture, and smell, every discussion of *vino* would begin and end with the same statement: "Tastes like wine!"

Likewise with visually perceived things, like color. Who decided that yellow was yellow, that blue was blue, and that light brownish-tan was taupe? Arbitrary, yes, but without such shared verbal designations, how would we be able to recognize and distinguish between different colors? (Oh, apropos of nothing: what are they feeding those nice folks who name the colors of Crayola Crayons? New colors include—and I kid you not—Manatee, Outer Space, Jazzberry Jam, Razzmatazz, and Beaver. Yes, Beaver. Learn to distinguish and identify those colors, my friends, and you'll have an eye!) But, to the point, terminology, properly defined and illustrated, goes hand-in-hand with our ability to identify and distinguish purely musical phcnomcna. Let's learn some words!

Beat or Pulse

The shortest, or smallest, time division to which we can comfortably move our bodies, to which we can comfortably dancc, is callcd the beat, or the pulse. We'll discuss that definition in a moment, but, first, let's listen to some music and let's find thc beat. I'm going to clap over the excerpt, and I want you to clap, or tap, your feet, or toes, or fingers, or whatever to that beat. This is not hard stuff; groove with me! Here we go—John Philip Sousa's *The Stars and Stripes Forever* of 1896. [**Musical selection:** John Philip Sousa, *The Stars and Stripes Forever* (1896)]

Now, we defined beat, or pulse, as being the shortest (or smallest) time division to which we can comfortably move our bodies, to which we can comfortably dance. This is obviously a subjective definition. Look, maybe you've had a long hard day and you're tired; perhaps that most comfortable time division for you, at this moment, is slower than the one I clapped. [**Musical selection:** John Philip Sousa, *The Stars and Stripes Forever* (1896); Professor Greenberg claps the beat slowly.] Or perhaps you're wired, having just consumed a triple espresso, with the result being that the most comfortable time division is rather more on the fast side. [**Musical selection:** John Philip Sousa, *The Stars and Stripes Forever* (1896); Professor Greenberg claps the beat fast.] I would suggest that if you can comfortably dance to that beat, you might consider cutting back on the caffeine, unless, of course, you are a gerbil. Tired or wired, the fact is that 99.99 percent of us will feel the same basic beat and will move our bodies to that beat in tandem. Listen, it's another conversation for another time, but we're hard-wired to react this way. Powerful beats affect us metabolically: Our heartbeats and respiration gravitate towards the speed of the beat, a beat that can coordinate group activity, be it social, sexual, work-related, ritual, whatever. The power of dance is primal and instinctive. It's a survival mechanism that allows us to coordinate our movements and activities with one another and with "the tribe."

The beat in music represents time, and once a beat is established in a piece of music—a process that takes only a few seconds—it becomes a continuum on which the entire musical structure rests, until a composer, or performer, chooses to somehow alter that beat, and thus create a new continuum. It's a constant source of amazement to me just how much musical and expressive information is contained within the beat in a given section of music: its relative strength, its speed, how certain beats are emphasized, or accented, and how beats are grouped, or not grouped! For example, I trust we had no problem finding and feeling the beat in John Philip Sousa's *The Stars and Stripes Forever*: it is strong and steady and of a moderate speed. Not only was its beat strong and steady, but we were hearing the beat grouped in sets of twos. Once more, let's hear the first minute of the march, and this time let's feel these groupings of two beats in your body: move to them, march to them! [**Musical selection:** John Philip Sousa, *The Stars and Stripes Forever* (1896); Professor Greenberg counts and claps to the beat.] We'll talk lots more about meter—that is, how beats are grouped—in our next lecture. For now, let's just be aware that we recognize John Philip Sousa's *The Stars and Stripes Forever* as a march because we perceived in it a steady series of moderately paced beats grouped in twos. I repeat: It's a constant source of amazement to me just how much musical and expressive information is transmitted via the beat in a given section of music.

Let's hear another piece of music. Our first task is to simply find a beat we are comfortable with and then move some part of our body, preferably something in the lower half, and by this I mean our feet. Okay! To the beat! Once we've found and gotten comfortable with the beat, our second task will be to identify its properties and then what those properties tell us about the expressive content of the piece of music as a whole. Onward, to Johannes Brahms's op. 39, no. 4 for piano, four hands. I'll begin to clap the beat about halfway through the excerpt—about 21 seconds in. [**Musical selection:** Johannes Brahms, Waltzes for Piano Four Hands, op. 39, no. 4 (1865)] Like the Sousa march, the beat here is as solid and as steady as can be. Like the Sousa march, this is body music, music meant to make us move. Unlike the Sousa march, the beats in the Brahms are not being grouped in twos, but rather, by threes. We'll discuss how these groupings are achieved in the next lecture. For now, I just want us to hear the Brahms excerpt again, and I will indicate the groupings by counting "three." All I expect from you, at this point, is to recognize that the beats in this music are indeed describing—defining—groups of three. [**Musical selection:** Johannes Brahms, Waltzes for Piano Four Hands, op. 39, no. 4 (1865)] So, what does the nature of the beat tell us about this piece? First, its power and clarity tell us that this music is rooted in dance, in physical movement. Second, its moderate speed and groupings in three tell us that it is a particular kind of dance, a three-step dance called a waltz.

Tempo

When we talk about the relative speed of a passage of music, we're talking about its *tempo*. *Tempo* means "time" in Italian and, gratefully, the terminological lexicon of musical tempo terms is in Italian. We say "gratefully" because Italian musical terms have two great assets: one, they actually sound like what they mean, and two, they're easy on both the ear and the tongue. To the former point—that they sound like what they mean—my friends, which of the following two words means "very slowly" and which means "very fast": *largo* and *presto*? Yes, *largo*, with its long vowel and relatively soft articulation sounds like molasses in January—slow and gooey—*largo*. Whereas, *presto*, with its shorter vowel, its sibilant "s" ("preSSto"), and its sharper consonants, simply sounds faster! Okay. How about *vivace* and *lento*? Which one means "lively" and the other "slowly"? Again, a no-brainer: the word *vivace* sounds lively; the word *lento* sounds lugubrious. But, as a word, *lento* still sounds good, yes? *Lento*. It falls easily on the ear and the tongue, as opposed to German. *Lento* in German is "*ganz langsam.*" *Largo* (very slowly) in German is "*ganz, ganz langsam.*" No, it's not pretty. Neither is "*Schnell!*" which means the same as *presto*, or the German equivalent of *vivace*, which is "*aufgeweckt.*"

The six basic tempo designations are, in decreasing order of speed: very fast (*presto*); fast (*allegro*); moderate, or walking speed (*andante*); moderately slow (*adagio*); slow (*lento*); very slow (*largo*). Again: *presto, allegro, andante, adagio, lento, largo*. Now, obviously, there are lots more Italian words that address this issue of tempo, although these six words comprise the vast majority of tempo markings we will encounter. Which presents a problem, a sometimes big problem.

I've just sat down at the piano and on the music stand is the first movement of Mozart's Piano Sonata in C Major of 1788. Above the first notes at the upper left-hand corner of the first page of the movement is the word *allegro* meaning "fast." My friends, how fast is *fast*? Should I play it this fast? [**Piano example:** Wolfgang Mozart, Piano Sonata in C Major, K. 545 (1788), movement 1, opening, played moderately fast] Or should I play it this fast? [**Piano example:** Wolfgang Mozart, Piano Sonata in C Major, K. 545 (1788), movement 1, opening, played faster] Or, perhaps, this fast? [**Piano example:** Wolfgang Mozart, Piano Sonata in C Major, K. 545 (1788), movement 1, opening, played faster still] The question: How fast is fast? When Mozart wrote *allegro* at the beginning of the piece, how a*llegro*—how fast did he want it to be played?

It's not just a good question, because when it comes to proper interpretation, matters of tempo are *the* question: determining the most appropriate tempo remains the single most important decision a performer can make, as well as an endless source of argument, rancor, and even blood-feuds between musicians. Ideally, Mozart would have qualified that designation of *allegro*; he would have given us more information. Rather than a genuine allegro, he probably meant an *allegretto*, or an *allegro moderato*, something a little less fast, something like this. [**Piano example:** Wolfgang Mozart, Piano Sonata in C Major, K. 545 (1788), movement 1, opening, played moderately fast] How do we know that's what Mozart probably wanted? Well, we don't know, not for sure. It's just that the piece sounds better at that tempo; it breathes and has a sense of pacing that seems appropriate to its melodic and harmonic material.

Eighty-five years later—in 1873—Johannes Brahms, doing his level best to be absolutely crystal clear as to the moderately fast tempo of the third movement of his String Quartet, op. 51, no. 1, indicated that the movement should be played *allegretto molto moderato e comodo*, which means, literally, "very kind of, sort of fast, but moderately and leisurely." Does that make any sense to any of you? Was Brahms being as clear as he wanted to be, or was he just further muddying the waters of tempo? I would tell you that *allegretto molto moderato e comodo* is just the sort of Brahmsian tempo designation that prompted the 20th-century American composer Carl Ruggles to ask: "What the hell is that supposed to mean?" Brahms should have used metronome markings. Why he didn't is anyone's guess. In 1815, a Viennese builder of mechanical musical instruments named

Johann Nepomuk Maelzel patented a device he called a metronome, a device that could be set to make a regular clicking sound anywhere from 40 to 200 times a minute. By using a metronome marking, a composer can indicate exactly the tempo of a piece of music, by indicating exactly how many clicks, or beats, should go by per minute.

Mozart, then, would have saved us all a lot of trouble had he lived long enough to own a metronome and had he marked his C-major Piano Sonata "quarter note = 116," meaning 116 beats per minute. Here's what that sounds like on a metronome. [**Metronome demonstration:** 116 beats per minute] And now I would play it at that tempo. [**Piano example:** Wolfgang Mozart, Piano Sonata in C Major, K. 545 (1788), movement 1, opening, played at 116 beats per minute] So comfortable and it would have been so specific. So, that settles it, right? If a composer employs a metronome marking, a performer will know, at the very least, how fast to start a piece of music! Yes, in an ideal world, performers would, indeed, honor a composer's metronome mark. Unfortunately, as we all know, we do not live in an ideal world. For example, Beethoven's Symphony no. 3 (the *Eroica* or *Heroic* Symphony) is about the trials and tribulations of a heroic, machismo character, who must overcome his inner demons as well as fate itself! In other words, Beethoven's Third is about Beethoven. The opening theme of the first movement, initially played by the 'cellos—the "baritone" voice of the orchestra—is the hero himself. Beethoven got himself a metronome and proceeded to write metronome marks into many of his works, including this third symphony. For the first movement of this third symphony, Beethoven indicated a tempo of dotted half note = 60, meaning that the piece should be played this fast and I reset the metronome. Here's Beethoven's indicated tempo. [**Metronome demonstration:** dotted half note = 60] And I'll play it at that tempo. [**Piano example:** Ludwig van Beethoven, Symphony no. 3 in Eb Major, op. 55 (*Eroica*, 1803), movement 1, played at dotted half note = 60] In a 1961 recording of Beethoven's third symphony, Conductor A, considered by many the great Beethoven conductor of the mid-20th century, begins the third symphony this way. How "heroic" does this feel? [**Musical selection:** Ludwig van Beethoven, Symphony no. 3 in Eb Major, op. 55 (*Eroica*, 1803), movement 1, opening] Well, that's a big snore. For your information, that conductor chose to begin the symphony at 46 beats per minute, nearly 25 percent slower than Beethoven's own metronome mark.

Now, in a 1994 recording of this same piece, Conductor B performed the same passage this way. [**Musical selection:** Ludwig van Beethoven, Symphony no. 3 in Eb Major, op. 55 (*Eroica*, 1803), movement 1, opening] Now, doesn't that feel better; doesn't that sound "heroic"? Yes, it does. It almost goes without saying that Conductor B has hit Beethoven's notated tempo spot on: 60 beats per minute. So, which conductor is right, Conductor A, or Conductor B? My friends, might I suggest that Beethoven is right, and clearly Conductor B has chosen to honor Beethoven's wishes. Now, if Conductor A were standing here, today, I've no doubt that he might make a good argument, perhaps even a compelling argument, in favor of his interpretation of the symphony, providing he didn't stick a sausage-like finger in my chest and tell me that if I didn't like it, I could blow it out my sackbut—behavior rather typical of the old-style, autocratic German conductor he was.

But, back to this conductor's interpretation and the question it begs: Does interpretive license extend to ignoring a composer's notated tempo? No, it does not. My friends, this is simply another example of the power of the living over the dead. Really, do any of us think that Conductor A would have conducted the *Eroica* at the tempo he did if Beethoven had been in the recording studio with him? We can hear Ludwig van now, shrieking from the back of the room: "You, you, yeah you, I'm talkin' to you, that's right you, the one with the stick! You messin' with my tempos? Don't you ever mess with my tempos!!!" Knowing Beethoven as we do, we would never, in his presence, mess with his tempos, and neither, I believe, would have Conductor A!

Period Instruments Versus Modern Instruments and the Right Tempo!

I'm still being asked, although not as often as I was fifteen years ago when this was still a hot button issue, as to whether I prefer recordings made with period instruments, or modern instruments. It's a fascinating thing, this period instrument revival we've seen in the last thirty years, and it deserves a much longer and more reasoned discussion than we have time to give it now. A few big statements before getting on to the point, which is tempo.

First, I've heard some wonderful period instrument recordings and I've heard some absolutely dreadful ones. I've heard some wonderful modern instrument recordings, and I've heard some that are so bad that I had to brush my teeth after having heard them, just to get the taste out of my mouth. As always in life, the means are important, but the end result is what matters. If a performer is willing to follow the one commandment—thou shalt honor the composer's wishes as best as can be divined—then a responsible performance is likely to be the result.

Period instrument zealots claim that we should hear Beethoven's music "the way Beethoven's own audience heard it." That argument assumes that there was a fixed instrumental standard in Beethoven's time, something we can copy and imitate today. Well, there wasn't. On top of that, the great bulk of the string and wind instruments available in Beethoven's time would have been much more likely to slip out of tune during the course of a performance than anything we'd hear on a modern recording. The quality of the instruments themselves would have been much less consistent than anything we'd hear on a recording. Likewise, the sheer level of musicianship we will hear on a modern recording will eclipse all but the greatest ensembles of Beethoven's day. If Beethoven could somehow hear the best modern recordings of his symphonies (and, for that matter, his piano sonatas and string quartets), I believe he'd be stunned—in his own lifetime, he would have never heard his music performed so well. Conversely, Johann Sebastian Bach had the opportunity to play an early piano, which he dismissed out-of-hand as being a toy. Does that mean we're supposed to ignore Glenn Gould's superb recordings of Bach's harpsichord music played on a modern grand piano? Now, speaking for myself, I will generally prefer a great period instrument recording to a great modern instrument recording, but, for me, it's not a matter of "hearing what Beethoven's audience heard," but, rather, of hearing what Beethoven wrote down on paper in terms of timbral balance, articulation, and tempo.

Timbral balance. Back to Beethoven's Symphony no. 3. Beethoven scored the symphony for two flutes, two oboes, two clarinets, two bassoons, three French horns, two trumpets, two timpani, and strings. In total, eight winds, five brass, timpani, and strings. Beethoven's string section would have numbered about 40 instruments, playing, incidentally, on gut rather than steel strings, resulting in an overall orchestral complement of 54 players, precisely the number employed by Conductor B. Let's hear the beginning of that performance again. [**Musical selection:** Ludwig van Beethoven, Symphony no, 3 in Eb Major, op. 55 (*Eroica*, 1803), movement 1, opening] Crisp and beautifully balanced, yes? Yes! We hear the winds and brass speak because they are not being drowned out by too many strings. As opposed to so many modern orchestra performances, in which an orchestra's entire string complement of over 60 stringed instruments is used in performance.

I'll be the first to admit it: Sixty-plus modern strings make a marvelous sound. But, those modern, steel-stringed instruments are bigger, louder, and less supple than those of Beethoven's day. Use too many of them in a performance and the 13 wind and brass instruments for which Beethoven also composed will not have a snowball's chance in Miami of being heard. In such a string-heavy performance, timbral balance goes right out the window, along with whatever essential musical material the winds and brass are playing.

Articulation and Tempo

Period strings are very different from modern instruments. As performance venues grew larger during the 19th century, the strings were modified to make them capable of playing louder. Steel and wound strings (strung at a higher tension) replaced gut strings. The thicker strings and higher tension required that the necks of the instruments be enlarged, the bridges made higher, the bodies reinforced, and the bows made bigger and more tautly strung. These changes did indeed make the strings capable of playing louder, but at the cost of flexibility. Period stringed instruments speak more rapidly and are capable of a lightness of attack and articulation that their modern cousins simply are not. Very simply, it's easier to play faster on period strings than modern strings and it's therefore easier to honor the sorts of faster tempos and articulations that were created with these instruments in mind in the first place!

Back to the Beat

All the beats we've observed thus far in this lecture have been steady and even and, as such, informed at a basic level by dance, that is, by physical movement. While we listen to the following excerpt, I will clap the beats. Feel free to clap and/or tap along if you wish. Here's the question: Are the beats in this music steady and even. If not, why not? [**Musical selection:** Harry von Tilzer and Joseph Lamb, *A Bird in a Gilded Cage* (1900)] Were the beats steady and even? Yeah, about as even as a hockey player's teeth. No, they weren't. The performance sped up and slowed down constantly. Why? The answer, my friends, is in the words:

The ballroom was filled with fashion's throng.
>It shone with a thousand lights;
>And there was a woman who passed along,
>The fairest of all the sights.
>A girl to her lover then softly sighed,
>"There's riches at her command";
>"But she married for wealth, not for love!"
>He cried, "Though she lives in a mansion grand!"

>She's only a bird in a gilded cage,
>A beautiful sight to see.
>You may think she's happy and free from care,
>She's not, though she seems to be.
>'Tis sad when you think of a wasted life,
>For youth cannot mate with age.
>And her beauty was sold
>For an old man's gold!
>She's a bird in a gilded cage!

Okay. Why wasn't the beat steady and even? Because our performance stresses the words and the story that the words tell. The tempo rises and falls with the natural rhetorical flow of story telling. This is a song and, in this particular performance of this particular song, the rhetorical element is more important than the dance element.

When the beat speeds up during the course of a passage, we call it an *accelerando*, which means, literally, "accelerating." When the beat slows down during the course of a passage, we called it a *ritardando*, or *ritard*, which means, literally, "slowing." Our performance of *A Bird in a Gilded Cage* is filled with *accelerandi* and *ritardandi*, as the performers take a very flexible, rhetorical approach to the beat. The term for such a free and flexible approach to the beat is called *rubato*. *Rubato* means, literally, "robbed time," as we steal from one beat (by shortening it) and give to another (by lengthening it), all in the name of lyric flexibility, in order to create a performance in which the rhetorical element is more important than the dance element.

The Polish-born composer and pianist Frédéric Chopin was famous for his rubato. Ear-witnesses to his piano playing in the 1830s and 1840s talk constantly about his uncanny ability to actually make the piano sing as a result of his incredibly nuanced approach to dynamics, phrase, and tempo. Take this Chopin Mazurka in A Minor I've got sitting on the piano, op. 17, no. 4 of 1833 as an example. A mazurka, like a waltz, is a three-step dance. Oh, sure, I could play it like a dance. [**Piano example:** Frédéric Chopin, Mazurka in A Minor, op. 17, no. 4, played as a dance] Sure, we could play it like a dance, and in doing so, miss entirely the expressive point of the piece. The piece is about aching, lyric melancholy; more than a dance, it is a song of regret. We must perform it with rubato, and in doing so, bring out its vocality, its essentially rhetorical nature. [**Piano example:** Frédéric Chopin, Mazurka in A Minor, op. 17, no. 4, played as a song of regret] Now, that's what Chopin's Mazurka in A Minor, op. 17, no. 4 is supposed to sound like, with a liquid flexibility of beat that renders it much more song than dance.

We've one more bit of "beat" business before we can bring this lecture to a close. Earlier in this lecture, we observed that in a given section of music, the beat, this smallest and most accessible of rhythmic elements, transmits a tremendous amount of musical and expressive information. This is particularly true if, in a given passage of music, the beat appears to be missing altogether! I would wax philosophic for just a moment. We homo sapiens perceive movement through time not as an unmarked continuum, but, rather, as being rooted in small, fairly even divisions. Now, I speak not of the ticking of a clock, or the hup-two of a Sousa march, but, rather, of our own heartbeats, our own built in metronomes for which the ticking of a clock is a metaphor and the steps in a march an analog. My friends, if a composer really wants to create tension—and here, we're talking about existential tension, ur-tension, mega-dislocation—what better way than by denying us that most essential, basic, and easily perceived element in any piece of music, meaning the beat!

Case in point: the overture to Richard Wagner's music drama *Tristan und Isolde* of 1859. During the first act of the drama, with a little help from some non-prescription pharmaceuticals, Tristan and Isolde fall madly in love with each other. They spend the remaining two and a half acts of the music drama vainly attempting to physically consummate that love. At its heart, *Tristan und Isolde* is about unrequited love; about the frustrating inability to physically consummate an overwhelming passion; about an itch that cannot be scratched. How does Wagner make us, as an audience, feel that same unrequited urge, that unscratchable itch during his overture? One of the ways he does it is by denying us any semblance of beat for the first two minutes plus! [**Musical selection:** Richard Wagner, *Tristan und Isolde* (1859), overture, opening] Yeah, that'll make you itch a little bit at the beginning of a five-hour evening, won't it? The overture was moving forward all along, but out-of-time, without any reference to a beat. So, when the music finally settles on something resembling a beat, a series of marked and perceivable time divisions to which our bodies can finally move, the relief, momentary though it might be, is physically palpable!

To answer the question: if there's no beat during the first two minutes of Wagner's overture to *Tristan und Isolde*, how is it notated? And how does the conductor manage to keep the players together? My friends, this is a case in which notation and perception are two very different things. On paper, the music looks entirely normal, with rhythms and beats meticulously indicated. But, we are told to play the music lento (ever so slowly) and there are long rests with signs called *fermatas* placed above them, fermatas that tell the conductor to pause for as long as she'd like. More than following the notated rhythms in their parts, the players are following the conductor's baton and that baton is telling them when to play and when not to play. Think of it all as an orchestral rubato, one in which time is so stretched out that we no longer perceive the beat so much as unrestricted temporal space. When we return: meter! Thank you.

Lecture Five
Meter, Part 1

Scope:
In this lecture, we consider two basic types of meter: duple and triple. Identifying meter is a physical process. Triple meter is, in essence, a dance meter. Most 17th-, 18th-, and 19th-century instrumental compositions set in triple meter are based on triple-meter dances, of which the waltz has enjoyed the most enduring popularity. Plainchant is an example of music that is not characterized by meter. To facilitate the reading and notation of music, measures and bar lines were invented and, by the late 17th century, were universally employed. Time signatures indicate the meter and the duration of the beat.

Outline

I. *Meter* refers to how individual beats are grouped in a given passage of music.

    A. We will learn to identify and recognize four basic types of meter: duple meter, triple meter, compound meter, and additive meter.

    B. Meter makes itself apparent through some sort of emphasis called *accent* or *accentuation*. Such accents usually occur regularly, most commonly creating patterns of two, three, or four beats.

        1. Duple meter is the occurrence of accented beats every two or four beats. **Musical selection**: Hector Berlioz, *Symphonie fantastique* (1830), movement 4.

        2. Accented beats occurring every three beats create triple meter. **Musical selection**: Johannes Brahms, Waltzes for Piano Four Hands, op. 39, no. 15 (1865).

    C. Accented beats are not necessarily louder than other beats.

        1. In Brahms's waltz, the "oom" in the "oom-pa-pa" is heard on notes lower than the "pa-pa." **Piano example**. That registral isolation—the lower notes—serves to emphasize them.

2. Accentuation can be a result of melodic phrase structure. **Musical selection**: Joseph Haydn, Symphony no. 94 in G Major (*Surprise*, 1791), movement 2, opening.
3. However they are emphasized, we perceive accented beats as being the first beat of whatever metric unit we are hearing. We call this first accented beat the *downbeat*. The beat that immediately precedes the downbeat is the *upbeat*.

D. Identifying meter is a physical process.
   1. First, we find the beat, then we "feel around" for the emphasis (accent), and in doing so, we sense whether the beats are being grouped in twos and fours (duple meter) or in threes (triple meter).
   2. The following excerpts are all in duple meter. **Musical selections**: Johann Sebastian Bach, *Brandenburg* Concerto no. 2 in F Major, BWV 1047 (c. 1719), movement 1, opening (repeated); Wolfgang Mozart, Clarinet Quintet in A Major, K. 581 (1789), movement 4 (repeated); Johannes Brahms, Quintet in B Minor for Clarinet and Strings, op. 115 (1891), movement 3, opening (repeated); Peter Ilyich Tchaikovsky, Symphony no. 4 in F Minor, op. 36 (1877), movement 4, opening (repeated).
   3. Once the beat and the meter are established, they continue until the composer alters them or stops them. This means that they continue through moments of silence. **Piano example**.

II. Triple meter is, at its essence, a dance meter. The overwhelming number of instrumental compositions in the 17th, 18th, and 19th centuries that are set in triple meter are based on triple-meter dances.

   A. The sarabande is a slow, stately dance in triple meter of Spanish origin. **Musical selection**: Johann Sebastian Bach, *Goldberg* Variations, BWV 988 (1741), theme.

   B. The minuet, a courtly three-step dance, was popular for more than 150 years from the mid-17th century through the early 19th century. It was the only Baroque-Era dance to find its way into the instrumental music of the Classical Era. **Musical selection**: Joseph Haydn, Symphony no. 100 in G

Major (*Military*, 1794), movement 3, opening.

C. The ländler is a slow-to-moderately-slow triple-meter dance of southern German and Austrian origin. Originally a peasant dance, it became popular in early-19th-century ballrooms until it was replaced by the waltz. **Musical selection**: Gustav Mahler, Symphony no. 1 in D Major (*Titan*, 1888), movement 2, opening.

D. The mazurka is a triple-meter Polish folk dance from the province of Mazovia, near Warsaw. Frédéric Chopin composed 51 mazurkas for solo piano that exhibit a huge range of expressive character. **Musical selection**: Frédéric Chopin, Mazurka in Bb Major, op. 7, no. 1 (1832).

E. The polonaise is another triple-meter Polish dance that Chopin made his own. His 16 polonaises for piano number among them some of the most justly popular and memorable music ever composed. **Musical selection**: Frédéric Chopin, Polonaise no. 3 in A Major, op. 40, no. 1 (*Military*, 1838).

F. The waltz has become virtually synonymous with triple meter.

    1. In terms of popularity, the waltz has bested even the minuet and has been the single most popular ballroom dance for the last 200 years.

    2. The waltz reached its zenith as a compositional genre in Vienna in the mid- and late 19th century, where the estimable Strauss family made it the preeminent popular music of its time. **Musical selection**: Johann Strauss II, *By the Beautiful Blue Danube* (1867).

    3. A Viennese waltz craze swept across America during the last years of the 19th century and the first years of the 20th century. The so-called songs of the Gay Nineties are almost all waltz songs in triple meter. **Piano examples**: John Palmer and Charles Ward, *The Band Played On* (1895); Chauncey Olcott, *My Wild Irish Rose* (1899); Henry Dacre, *Daisy* (1892); Charles Lawlor and James Blake, *Sidewalks of New York* (1894); Warren Shields and M. George Evans, *In the Good Old Summertime* (1902); Effie Canning, *Rock-a-bye Baby* (1886); Albert von Tilzer and Jack Norworth, *Take Me Out to the Ball Game*; Patty and Mildred Hill, *Happy Birthday* (1893).

G. Not all music is characterized by meter. Plainchant, the liturgical music of the medieval church, for example, is unmeasured. **Musical selection**: *Pange lingua* (c. 1270).

    1. The purpose of plainchant was to uplift the soul by intensifying prayer; thus, the musical rhythms are strictly a function of the words being sung.

    2. A strong patterned beat was perceived by the church as being a function of dance, which was considered to be the devil's playground. Hence, plainchant generally has no perceptible meter.

III. Although we are not relying on musical notation in this course, we will discuss its evolution and how it works.

A. A true instrumental tradition that made a distinction among solo music, chamber music, and orchestral music, and that saw composers create music specifically for these evolving media, did not appear until the Baroque Era during the mid-1600s.

B. To facilitate the reading and notation of the dance meters that lay at the heart of the great bulk of Baroque instrumental music, measures (bars) and bar lines came into regular use during the mid-17th century and, by the late 17th century, were almost universal.

    1. A measure or bar is a notational device for indicating one metric unit of music.

    2. If, for example, a piece of music is in triple meter, every metric unit of three beats equals one measure; one measure in triple meter is three beats. **Piano example**: four groups of triple meter, four measures long.

    3. Bar lines are notational devices: two vertical lines that enclose a measure—that is, one metric unit.

C. A time signature is a notational device that indicates the meter. Time signatures look like fractions. The top number indicates the meter (how many beats there are in each metric unit or measure). The bottom number indicates what sort of note gets one beat.

    1. If the top number is a 3, the music is in triple meter.

    2. If the top number is a 2 or a 4, the music is in duple meter.

Lecture Five—Transcript
Meter, Part 1

This is Lecture Five. It is entitled "Meter, Part 1." We resume our exploration of the time aspect of music with meter. Meter refers to how individual beats are grouped in a given passage of music. There are four basic types of meter we will identify and learn to recognize: duple meter, triple meter, compound meter, and additive meter.

Accent

The meter of a given section of music makes itself apparent through some sort of emphasis called an accent. Such accents will usually occur regularly, most commonly creating patterns of two, three, or four, beats. When we hear accented beats occurring every two, or four, beats—and thereby creating a pattern, or meter, of two, or four—we say that the music is in duple meter. For example, Hector Berlioz's famous "March to the Scaffold" from the fourth movement of his *Symphonie fantastique* of 1830. [**Musical selection:** Hector Berlioz, *Symphonie fantastique* (1830), movement 4; Professor Greenberg counts the beats.] When we hear accented beats occurring every three beats, and thereby creating a pattern, or meter, of three, we say the music is in triple meter. For example, Johannes Brahms's Waltz, op. 39, no. 15 of 1865. [**Musical selection:** Johannes Brahms, Waltzes for Piano Four Hands, op. 39, no. 15 (1865); Professor Greenberg counts the beats.]

Now, it's a fallacy to assume that accented beats are perceived as being accented because they are louder. Yes, in Berlioz's "March to the Scaffold," the accented beats were slightly louder than the unaccented beats, something typical of a march. But, accentuation (emphasis) can occur any number of different ways. For example, in a waltz—and this was true in the Brahms waltz we just heard—the "oom" in the "oom-pa-pa" is typically heard on notes lower than the "pah-pah." [**Piano example**] That registral isolation—the lower notes on "oom"—serves to emphasize "oom" and thus we perceive it as being accented. Accentuation can be a result of melodic phrase structure. For example, the second movement of Haydn's Symphony no. 94 of 1791 begins with a melody whose phrases are each four beats long. As a result, we perceive the beat that falls at the beginning of each of those phrases as being emphasized, or accented.

[**Musical selection:** Joseph Haydn, Symphony no. 94 in G Major (*Surprise*, 1791), movement 2, opening; Professor Greenberg counts the beats.]

However they are emphasized, we perceive these regularly accented beats as being the first beat of whatever metric unit we're hearing. Therefore, we call this first, accented beat the downbeat, because we feel in its emphasis a downward thrust into mother earth, into gravity central. That's no metaphor. My friends, when we dance, or tap our toes, or march, we naturally thrust our weight downwards on the downbeat, as if to physically anchor ourselves at this moment of greatest rhythmic weight. Conversely, the beat that immediately precedes the downbeat is called the upbeat, for the obvious reason that it prepares the downward thrust that follows.

Learning to Identify Duple and Triple Meter

My friends, sadly there's no science, or theory, to identifying meter. We just practice, and eventually, like the Crayola Crayon maven who can instantly identify that particular shade called Wild Blue Yonder, we just know what meter we're in when we hear it. The steps to identifying meter are as follows. Step one: We find the beat. When finding a beat, we do not think, reason, or try to figure it out. On the contrary, we dance in place; we let go; we allow our bodies to tell us where the beat is. Oh yes, I know, I know. This is so antithetical to the sort of intellectual engagement we're accustomed to when we learn new stuff, but this is music, not statistics, and very often, learning something about music is about becoming conscious of something we instinctively knew already, like moving to a beat! Step one, then, in learning to identify duple and triple meter: Find the beat. Step two—and here we go again, I feel badly about this, I really do—step two is to feel around for emphasis, for accent, and in doing so, sense whether the beats are being grouped in twos, or fours (which would be duple meter), or threes (which would be triple meter). Again, this is not an intellectual, but, rather, a physical process. It's about finding a comfortable beat and then allowing the beat to tell us how it is being grouped: in twos, threes, or fours.

Look, my friends, before we start practicing, a necessary pep talk. I suggest a scenario. You're at a wedding reception. The band plays the first dance; first, the bride and her father, then the groom and his mother move onto the dance floor and begin to dance a waltz, a three-step. You and your partner walk onto the floor and, likewise, whether clumsily, or gracefully, dance a three-step. Did anyone have to tell you that the piece was in triple meter and that the appropriate dance would be something involving three steps? No. You felt it. Next, the band strikes up a swing number. Swing, by definition, is duple- meter music. You begin to step in groups of two and/or four. No one has to tell you the music is in duple meter. No. You just felt it and don't tell me you have two left feet. Aside from Gerald Fleck in the movie *Best in Show*, I've never seen anyone with two left feet, nor a pianist with two right hands, much as we'd all like to have two right hands.

But, to the point: We've been listening to music our entire lives. We've been hearing and moving and dancing to music in duple and triple meter our entire lives. When we get to pitch, and melody, and tonality, and harmony, we'll be talking about aspects of music that, likewise, we've been hearing our entire lives. What we're doing, in this course, is not so much learning new stuff as: one, making ourselves consciously aware of musical aspects we've been intuitively aware of our entire lives and two, creating a vocabulary that allows us to observe and address these aspects in detail.

Practice Makes Perfect—Duple Meter

All the following musical examples are in duple meter. We will listen to each excerpt twice. During the first listening, I will be uncharacteristically silent. What I want us to do is: one, dance, find the beat and two, feel around for accentuation. Those accents will allow us to count the beats in groups of two or four. For our purposes it makes no difference which. We will then hear each excerpt again, during which time I will clap what I consider the primary beat and will count out loud the meter. We begin with the first movement of Johann Sebastian Bach's *Brandenburg* Concerto no. 2 in F Major of circa 1719. [**Musical selection:** Johann Sebastian Bach, *Brandenburg* Concerto no. 2 in F Major, BWV 1047 (c. 1719), movement 1, opening] Okay; let's count the Bach together. I'm going to count it in four, and let's be aware of how truly four-square this music is, as instrumental solos and other such events line up exactly with the count of four. [**Musical selection:** Johann Sebastian Bach, *Brandenburg* Concerto no. 2 in F Major, BWV 1047 (c. 1719), movement 1, opening]

Let's next hear the opening of the fourth and final movement of Mozart's fabulous Clarinet Quintet of 1789. Again, first find the beat and then feel around for accentuation. [**Musical selection:** Wolfgang Mozart, Clarinet Quintet in A Major, K. 581 (1789), movement 4, opening] We can comfortably count this music in either two or four, depending upon whether we're feeling a relatively fast beat, or a relatively slow beat. I'm going to forego the clapping this time around and, instead, I'll first count in two and then in four, with the understanding that, either way, it's still duple meter. [**Musical selection:** Wolfgang Mozart, Clarinet Quintet in A Major, K. 581 (1789), movement 4, opening]

While we're listening to clarinet quintets, that is, works for one clarinet and four strings, let's turn to the other great masterwork of the genre, Johannes Brahms's Clarinet Quintet in B Minor of 1891. Let's hear the opening of the third movement, which is marked *andantino*, meaning "a little bit faster than walking speed." First find the beat, then feel around, my friends, for accentuation. [**Musical selection:** Johannes Brahms, Quintet for Clarinet and Strings in B Minor, op. 115 (1891), movement 3, opening] Again, we could count this in either two or four depending on our mood and, even more importantly, depending on the performance. As it is, Brahms notated it in four, though again, what's important is that we perceive duple meter. [**Musical selection:** Johannes Brahms, Quintet for Clarinet and Strings in B Minor, op. 115 (1891); movement 3, opening; Professor Greenberg counts the beats.]

One more example of duple meter before we move on: the opening of the fourth and final movement of Tchaikovsky's Symphony no. 4 of 1877. Tchaikovsky indicates that this movement be played *allegro con fuoco* (fast and with fire). Again, first find the beat, and don't be put off, my friends, by the rests that appear here and there at the beginning of the excerpt. Once the beat is established, it continues non-stop, just like our own heartbeats, whether we're hearing music, or silence! [**Musical selection:** Peter Ilyich Tchaikovsky, Symphony no. 4 in F Minor, op. 36 (1877), movement 4, opening] Tchaikovsky notated this in four, but we are going to count it in two. Why? Because I'm feeling more like two right now. So, here we go. "Fast and with fire!" [**Musical selection:** Peter Ilyich Tchaikovsky, Symphony no. 4 in F Minor, op. 36 (1877), movement 4, opening; Professor Greenberg counts the beats.]

An important point, one I would now reinforce. Before we listened to the Tchaikovsky for the first time, I pointed out that a steady beat is a continuum; once established, it continues as a non-stop given, as the basic rhythmic underpinning, whether we're hearing music or silence. We need to be clear on this because it's very important: Once the beat and the meter are established—something that takes only a few seconds—we sense their presence as a given until the composer alters them, or stops them. For example, count to four along with me and continue counting while I play at the piano. [**Piano example**] Did the beat and meter stop during the silences in the music? No they did not! On the contrary, once established, our bodies will continue to perceive, to resonate with whatever beat and meter have been established until a composer chooses to alter, or stop them entirely.

Triple Meter

Triple meter is, at its essence, a dance meter. It is a fact that the overwhelming number of 17th-, 18th-, and 19th-century instrumental compositions set in triple meter are based on triple-meter dances. Let this be the hook for our investigation of triple meter: let's examine movements, or entire compositions, based on triple-meter dances: the sarabande, the minuet, the ländler, the mazurka, the polonaise, and the waltz.

Triple-Meter Dances—The Sarabande

We start, my friends, with the theme of what must be considered one of the greatest compositions of all time: Johann Sebastian Bach's The *Goldberg* Variations of 1741. The theme, from which Bach will create 30 of the most miraculous variations ever conceived, is a sarabande, a slow, stately dance in triple meter of Spanish origin. Let's hear the first two phrases of the theme. I will remain silent during the first phrase, and will count during the second phrase. Please, let's feel the rocking sense of motion that is such a marked element of triple meter, particularly at a slow tempo. [**Musical selection:** J. S. Bach, *Goldberg* Variations, BWV 988 (1741), theme]

Triple-Meter Dances—The Minuet

The stunning popularity and longevity of the minuet still amazes us today. It was the courtly three-step dance of choice for more than

150 years, from the mid-17th century through the early 19th century. Moderate in tempo and stately in mood, the minuet is also the only Baroque-Era dance to find its way into the instrumental music of the Classical Era. During the Classical Era, a minuet appeared as the second, or third movement of almost every four-movement composition, placed there to offer a metric contrast with the duple-meter movements that typically surrounded it. As an example, let's hear the opening of the third-movement minuet from Haydn's Symphony no. 100 of 1794. Once again, I'll remain silent during the first part of the excerpt, and will count during the second part. Again, find the beat, feel for accentuation, then start counting threes. [**Musical selection:** Joseph Haydn, Symphony no. 100 in G Major (*Military*, 1794), movement 3, opening]

Triple-Meter Dances—The Ländler

The ländler is a slow-to-moderate triple-meter dance of southern German and Austrian origin. Originally a peasant dance, it became quite popular in the early 19th century in Germany and Austria until it was replaced by the waltz. One of the charms of the ländler is that it never lost its peasant roots, so we should expect a certain rusticity from any movement called a ländler, like the second movement of Gustav Mahler's Symphony no. 1 of 1888. Let's count this one together, from the beginning. [**Musical selection:** Gustav Mahler, Symphony no. 1 in D Major (*Titan*, 1888), movement 2, opening]

Triple-Meter Dances—The Mazurka

The mazurka is a triple-meter Polish folk dance from the province of Mazovia, near Warsaw. While many Polish composers composed mazurkas, the shortlist of great "mazurkists" has but one name on it—Frédéric Chopin—and while Chopin's 51 mazurkas for solo piano exhibit a huge range of expressive character—witness the lyric, melancholy and not-at-all dance-like mazurka in A minor we discussed in Lecture Four—well, they are all, still, nevertheless, mazurkas. For a more dance-like example, we turn to Chopin's Mazurka in Bb Major, op. 7, no. 1 of 1832. Let's count it together. [**Musical selection:** Frédéric Chopin, Mazurka in Bb Major, op. 7, no. 1 (1832)]

Triple-Meter Dances—The Polonaise

Yet another triple-meter Polish dance type that Chopin made his very own is the polonaise. Chopin's 16 polonaises for piano number among them some of the most justly popular and memorable music ever composed, music that has become a national symbol for his native Poland. We sample Chopin's Polonaise in A Major, op. 40, no. 1, the so-called *Military* Polonaise, composed in 1838. We count together. [**Musical selection:** Frédéric Chopin, Polonaise No. 3 in A Major, op. 40, no. 1 (*Military*, 1838)]

Triple-Meter Dances—The Waltz

We conclude this discussion of dance-inspired triple meter music with the waltz, a dance that has become virtually synonymous with triple meter. Yes, rather annoyingly, triple meter is often referred to simply as waltz time, as if all the other triple-meter dance types we've discussed, and others that we haven't discussed, are nothing but musical chopped liver! In terms of longevity and popularity, the waltz has bested even the minuet. It has been the single most popular ballroom dance for the last two hundred years, and its popularity shows no sign of waning! The waltz reached its zenith as a compositional genre in mid- and late-19th-century Vienna, where the estimable Strauss family, Johann Strauss Senior and his son, Johann Strauss the Second, made the waltz the pre-eminent popular and concert music of its time. Of this father-son duo, it was Johann Strauss Junior, who was, by far, the greater composer. He was, in fact, one of the greatest composers of the 19th century. Yes, he wrote what is called in the literature light music, but his *Emperor* Waltz, his *Tales from the Vienna Woods*, and his *By the Beautiful Blue Danube*, and the operetta *Die Fledermaus* are, for what they are, creations of genius and mine is not a solitary opinion. The curmudgeonly Johannes Brahms worshiped the music of his friend Johann Strauss the Second, and said so at every opportunity. Richard Strauss (no relation to Johann) offered this appreciation later in his life: "Of all the god-gifted dispensers of joy, Johann Strauss [Junior] is to me the most endearing. In particular, I respect in Johann Strauss his originality, his innate gift. At a time when the whole world around him was tending towards increased complexity, his natural genius allowed him to create from the [heart]. He seemed to me the last of those [composers] who worked from spontaneous inspiration. I got to know and love his [genius] through [the pianist] Hans von Bülow, who had a beautifully bound copy of the Strauss waltzes. He played them for me [for] an entire evening. For me alone! An unforgettable evening of waltzes! As for [my own] *Rosenkavalier* Waltzes: how could I have composed them without thinking of the laughing genius of Vienna?!" (Schonberg Lives, third edition, 318)

All right, no counting this time around, my friends. Let's just kick back and enjoy: Johann Strauss the Second, "the Waltz King," a bit of *By the Beautiful Blue Danube* of 1867. [**Musical selection:** Johann Strauss II, *By the Beautiful Blue Danube* (1867)] Johann Strauss Junior's waltzes were almost as beloved in the United States as they were in Vienna. A Viennese waltz-craze swept America during the last years of the 19th and first years of the 20th century, a craze that only came to an end in 1917, when the United States declared war on Germany and the Austrian Empire. It was a waltz-craze that powerfully affected music being written in America, particularly popular songs.

The so-called songs of the Gay Nineties (meaning the carefree and happy 1890s; there's no sexual connotation intended in that phrase!), the songs of the Gay Nineties constitute a body of repertoire that's almost instantly recognizable and what almost all of these instantly recognizable songs have in common—like *A Bird in a Gilded Cage*—is they are so-called waltz songs—songs set in triple meter. What's remarkable is just how many of these waltz songs have attained an almost folk-song like status. A little waltz-song medley for your listening pleasure! We begin with John Palmer and Charles Ward's *The Band Played On* of 1895. [**Piano example**] Chauncey Olcott, *My Wild Irish Rose* of 1899. [**Piano example**] *Daisy* by Henry Dacre, 1892. [**Piano example**] Charles Lawlor and James Blake's *The Sidewalks of New York* of 1894. [**Piano example**] Warren Shields and M. George Evans's *In the Good Old Summertime* of 1902. [**Piano example**] Effie Canning's *Rock-a-bye Baby* of 1886. [**Piano example**]

The next song has words by Jack Norworth and music by Albert von Tilzer. Albert von Tilzer was the younger brother of Harry von

Tilzer, who wrote *A Bird in a Gilded Cage*. Albert and Harry's real last name was Gumm (spelled G-u-m-m). They were born to Jewish immigrant parents named Jacob and Sarah Gummbinsky. Tilzer was their mother's maiden name; the "von," well, the "von" was their little attempt to distance themselves from their humble ethnic beginnings, shall we say. My friends, in those days, no one in the entertainment industry kept their real name, especially if it was going to make them sound like some yiddisher greenhorn from the old country. Just so: Israel Balinsky became Irving Berlin; Jacob Gershovitz became George Gershwin; Aaron Kaplan became Aaron Copland. Oh, and it didn't end there. In the generations that followed, Allan Koenigsberg became Woody Allen, Bette Perske became Lauren Bacall; Melvin Kaminsky became Mel Brooks; Leonard Schneider became Lenny Bruce; Bernie Schwartz became Tony Curtis; Jack Cohen became Rodney Dangerfield; Danielovitch Demsky became Kirk Douglas; Robert Zimmerman became Bob Dylan; Eugene Horowitz became Michael Landon; Joseph Levitch became Jerry Lewis; Wolf Marvin Garber became Bill Macy; Winona Horowitz became Winona Ryder; the list goes on, we will not. Anyway, at the time Albert von Tilzer wrote the following waltz song in 1908, he had never even been to a baseball game. It made no difference; the song has become an American anthem. [**Piano example:** Albert von Tilzer and Jack Norwoth, *Take Me Out to the Ball Game* (1908)] Finally, let's hear what is certainly the best-known American waltz-song of all time, with music written in 1893 by the sisters Patty and Mildred Hill, a couple of school teachers from Louisville, Kentucky [**Piano example:** Patty and Mildred Hill, *Happy Birthday* (1893)]

A Caveat

Not all music will be characterized by meter. Plainchant, or so-called Gregorian Chant—the liturgical music of the medieval Catholic Church—is, for example, unmeasured. Let's listen to a plainchant setting of Thomas Aquinas' poem *Pange lingua* ("Sing, my tongue"), a relatively late plainchant, created around 1270. [**Musical selection:** Plainchant, *Pange lingua* (c. 1270)] The reasons behind the unmeasured nature of plainchant are both practical and political. First, the early church fathers held that the purpose of music was to uplift the soul by intensifying prayer, meaning that in plainchant, musical rhythms are strictly a function of the words being set to music. Second, a strong and patterned beat was perceived as being a function of dance, and dance was perceived as the devil's playground! The church eventually shifted its stance on pulsed, or measured music (what in Latin is called *musica mensurabilis*), but it took a long time for that to happen!

Notating Meter—Measures, Bar Lines, and Time Signatures

Now, just because we're not relying on music notation in this course doesn't mean we won't explain something of its evolution and how it works. Let's consider this as the first installment of an investigation into musical notation: notating meter—measures, bar lines, and time signatures. It was during the 17th century (the 1600s) that a genuine instrumental musical tradition truly began to develop. Now, obviously, instrumental music had existed before the 17th century, primarily in the form of dance music and arrangements of dance music. But, a true instrumental tradition, one that made a distinction between solo music, chamber music, and orchestral music, and one that saw composers create music specifically for these evolving instrumental genres, did not appear until the Baroque Era, specifically, the mid-1600s. In order to facilitate the reading and notation of meter, measures (or bars) and bar lines came into regular use during the mid-17th century. Measures and bar lines were such a great idea that they became almost universal—in instrumental and vocal music—by the late 17th century.

A measure, or bar, is a notational device for indicating one metric unit of music. For example, let's say we're in triple meter. Every metric unit of three beats equals one measure; one measure in triple meter is three beats. Here, I'll play four groups of triple meter. **[Piano example]** We would say that that excerpt is four measures long, since there were four measures (four units, four groups) of triple meter. On these lines, in terms of sheer number of measures, the longest movement of instrumental music Mozart ever composed is the fourth movement of his String Quintet in C Major of 1787. The movement is 537 measures long. The movement is notated in *two*, meaning that there are two beats in each metric unit. Therefore, the whole movement is 1,074 beats in length, two beats times 537 measures. Bar lines are a notational device: They are the two vertical lines that enclose a measure, that is, one metric unit.

A time signature is a notational device that indicates the meter. Time signatures look just like fractions, with one number written above another. Appearances notwithstanding, fractions they are not. The two numbers in a time signature tell us two very different things. The top number tells us how many beats there are in each metric unit (in each measure) and the bottom number tells us what sort of note gets a beat. For example: let's say that the top number is three and the bottom number is four, a meter we would therefore call three-four, or three-quarter time. The three on top tells us that there are three beats in each metric unit —that the meter is triple. The bottom number (the four) tells us that a quarter note gets one beat.

Now, this bottom number and the information it specifies—that a quarter note gets a beat—is vital if one is reading the music, but it is almost entirely irrelevant if one is simply listening to the music. Whether it's a quarter note, a half note, an eighth note, or a whatever-note that gets that beat, what's important, for the listener, is that we perceive three of them as making up a metric unit and therefore that we perceive triple meter. So, it's the top number in a time signature, the one that tells us how many beats are in each metric unit, in each measure, that is, for us, for now, the important number. If that number is a two, or a four, the music is in duple meter. If that number is a three, dollars-to-doughnuts says the music is in triple meter (with the exception of movements that are played so fast that we can't feel the threes as the primary beat, something we'll talk about in the next lecture). If that number on top is a five, or a seven, or a 10, or an 11, it means we are in additive meter, which is, again, something we'll talk about in the next lecture. I think it's time to bring this lecture to its conclusion. When we resume, we will talk about metric consistency and continue our discussion of meter. Thank you.

Lecture Six
Meter, Part 2

Scope:
Syncopation, which is the accentuation of beats that are not downbeats, can take the form of unpatterned or patterned accents. A pattern of syncopations, called a *hemiola*, can give the impression that the meter has actually changed. Compound meter features the subdivision of a beat into three and includes compound duple meter and compound triple meter. Additive meter is a combination of twos and threes. Asymmetrical meter is characterized by no repeated metric pattern.

Outline

I. In music of the Common Practice Period (c. 1600–1900), the meter of a particular movement tends to stay the same from the beginning to the end. In the 20th century, changing meter became common and remains so.

II. A syncopation is an accent where we do not expect an accent. Because we expect accents on downbeats, syncopations are accents on beats other than the downbeat or even in between beats.

    A. Syncopation can take two forms:

        1. It can be an accent or series of unpatterned accents at moments other than the downbeat, used to create a sense of rhythmic interest, ambiguity, and tension.

        2. A pattern of syncopations might be employed to momentarily change the meter during a given passage of music.

    B. In the minuet from his String Quartet, op. 18, Beethoven accents the third beat instead of the first beat to create musical excitement in what was, for Beethoven, an increasingly obsolescent musical genre, namely, the minuet. **Musical selection**: Ludwig van Beethoven, String Quartet no. 4 in C Minor, op. 18 (1799), movement 3, opening.

    C. Ragtime is a synthesis of vastly different elements, some of western European origin and some of West African origin.

1. In ragtime, the complex multiple rhythmic layers of West African drumming are transferred to the piano, with a march-like, on-the-beat left hand of the pianist supporting an off-the-beat, syncopated right hand layered atop.

2. The following excerpt illustrates syncopation used as an accent or series of unpatterned accents on moments other than the downbeat. **Musical selection**: Scott Joplin, *Maple Leaf Rag* (1899), opening.

3. Syncopation can also effect a temporary change of meter. In the following demonstration, a pattern of syncopations, called a *hemiola*, gives the impression of a change of meter from triple to duple meter. **Demonstration of meter. Musical selection**: Ludwig van Beethoven, Symphony no. 3 in Eb Major, op. 55 (*Eroica*, 1803), movement 1, opening.

4. This rhythmic ambiguity returns with a vengeance at the climactic moment of the movement. This is as brutal as Beethoven's musical language will allow him to be, and even today, this passage shocks. **Musical selection**: Ludwig van Beethoven, Symphony no. 3 in Eb major, op. 55 (*Eroica*, 1803), movement 1, development.

5. Beethoven was one of the most rhythmically inventive composers who ever lived. He isolated and manipulated rhythm in a way that was unique in his time. Indeed, his rhythmic audacity is very much of the 21st century.

III. A compound meter is any meter that features a triple subdivision within each beat.

   A. When the beats grouped in threes are too fast to be considered as being the primary beats, we hear each three-note grouping as constituting a single beat. **Musical selection**: Johannes Brahms, Trio in Eb Major for Violin, Piano and Horn, op. 40 (1865), movement 4, opening (repeated).

   B. A meter in which the primary beats are subdivided into very fast groups of three is called a compound meter because it is a composite of two different rhythmic levels: a primary beat subdivided into a fast group of three. **Musical selection**: Johannes Brahms, Trio in Eb Major for Violin, Piano, and

Horn, op. 40 (1865), movement 4, opening.

C. The particular meter that we hear in Brahms's trio is called compound duple meter because the primary beat is in duple. **Demonstration of meter**. **Musical selection**: Johannes Brahms, Trio in Eb Major for Violin, Piano and Horn, op. 40 (1865), movement 4, opening.

D. The following excerpt is another example of compound duple meter. **Demonstration of meter**. **Musical selection**: Johann Sebastian Bach, *Brandenburg* Concerto no. 6 in Bb Major, BWV 1051 (c. 1721).

   1. The time signature for compound duple meter is usually 6 over 8 (6/8 time), meaning that there are two fast groups of three or six eighth notes in every metric unit.

   2. The following excerpt is also an example of compound duple meter. **Musical selection**: Ludwig van Beethoven, Symphony no. 7 in A Major, op. 92 (1812), movement 1, theme 1.

E. There is also such a meter as compound triple. **Demonstration of meter**. **Musical selection**: Johann Sebastian Bach, Two-Part Invention no. 10 in G Major, BWV 781 (1723), opening.

F. By definition, any meter perceived as being a compound meter will be fast in tempo. **Piano example**: Johann Sebastian Bach, Two-Part Invention no. 10 in G Major, BWV 781 (1723), opening.

   1. We perceive this as a compound meter because the triplet subdivisions of the beat are too fast to feel as the primary beats.

   2. But if we play fast compound triple meter slowly enough, one measure will eventually sound like three measures of regular triple meter. **Demonstration of meter**. **Piano examples**: Johann Sebastian Bach, Two-Part Invention no. 10 in G Major, BWV 781 (1723), opening, played fast and compared with a slower tempo.

   3. Thus, to be properly perceived as being compound, the tempo must be fast enough that the triplet subdivisions will be perceived as subdivisions and not as primary beats.

4. Conversely, if a composer assigns a time signature of three-quarter time, then marks the movement *molto vivace* ("very lively" or "very fast"), we will not perceive it as being triple meter. **Musical selection**: Ludwig van Beethoven, Symphony no. 9 in D Minor, op. 125 (1824), movement 2, opening.

5. In fact, conductors do not conduct this movement in "three" but in "one." There is no special term for a meter like this; there is no such term as *compound single*! It's simply fast triple meter, conducted as if it were one beat subdivided into a fast triplet.

IV. Additive meter is some combination of twos and threes.

    A. The following excerpt is an example of a meter of five beats arrayed as a three plus a two. **Musical selection**: Peter Ilyich Tchaikovsky, Symphony no. 6 in B Minor, op. 74 (1893), movement 2, opening (repeated). This movement has been called the "Five-Legged Waltz"; it sounds like a waltz and feels like a waltz, but it is missing a beat every other measure.

    B. Additive meter is common in eastern European folk traditions, but until the 20th century, it was virtually unheard of in western European music.

    C. Modest Mussorgsky begins his *Pictures at an Exhibition* of 1874 with a movement entitled "Promenade." It starts with a fanfare consisting of four metric units of 11 beats each, spelled out in the score as a 5 plus a 6. **Musical selection**: Modest Mussorgsky, *Pictures at an Exhibition* (1874), "Promenade," opening.

        1. About halfway through the piece, the additive meter that characterized the first "Promenade" goes into hyperdrive as Mussorgsky mixes and matches many different meters.

        2. This "Promenade" begins like the first one, with four units of 11, each spelled out as a 5 plus a 6, but it continues differently: 11 + 11+ 11+ 11+ 6 + 6 + 11 + 6 + 11 + 6 + 6 + 7 + 7 + 11 + 11 + 11. **Musical selection**: Modest Mussorgsky, *Pictures at an Exhibition* (1874), "Promenade."

V. Mussorgsky's score indicates that the music should be played "in Russian style." This refers to rhythmic asymmetry that is characteristic of the Russian language and Russian folk music.

  A. Igor Stravinsky's *The Rite of Spring* (1912) offers a supreme example of metric asymmetry.

  B. The conclusion of an episode entitled "The Game of the Abduction" calls for these different meters: $3 + 5 + 5 + 3 + 4 + 5 + 6 + 5 + 2 + 6 + 6 + 6 + 6 + 2 + 6 + 4 + 6 + 6 + 4 + 6 + 6 + 6 + 4 + 2$. **Musical selection**: Igor Stravinsky, *The Rite of Spring* (1912), "The Game of the Abduction," conclusion.

  C. Additive meter should be not confused with metric asymmetry.

   1. Unlike additive meter, metric asymmetry (as in *The Rite of Spring*) exhibits no regularly repeated metric pattern.

   2. In the 20th and 21st centuries, asymmetrical meter became part of the common syntax of composed music.

VI. In the 20th century, Dave Brubeck and Paul Desmond created a body of music employing additive meter.

  A. Paul Desmond's famous *Take Five* employs a meter of five beats, with the beats arrayed as a three plus two.

  B. Dave Brubeck's *Blue Rondo à la Turk* of 1959 is neither a rondo nor very "blue" (as in *blues-like*); Brubeck claimed that the additive rhythms he used in the piece were inspired by folk music he heard on tour in Turkey.

   1. The theme is set in nine beats, subdivided in two different ways. **Demonstration**: | | 1–2 | 1–2 | 1–2 | 1–2–3 | | (repeated). **Piano example**: metric pattern as above.

   2. Every fourth measure (every fourth metric unit), Brubeck changes the way he subdivides the nine beats, going from | | 1–2 | 1–2 | 1–2 | 1–2–3 | | to | | 1–2–3 | 1–2–3 | 1–2–3 | |. **Demonstration of meter** followed by **musical selection**: Dave Brubeck, *Blue Rondo à la Turk* (1959), opening.

   3. Because the piece is played fast, Brubeck's groups of two can be felt as a single "short" beat and the groups of three as a single "long" beat. **Demonstration of meter**.

   4. Brubeck saves his best rhythmic trick for last. At almost two minutes into the piece, the music begins alternating back and forth between | 1–2 | 1–2 | 1–2 | 1–2 | 1–2–3 | and straight, swinging duple meter in which the beats are the same length as the "long" | 1–2–3 |. **Demonstration**:

|| 1–2 | 1–2 | 1–2 | 1–2–3 | || (repeated 3 times)
|| 1–2–3 | 1–2–3 | 1–2–3 | ||
|| 1–2–3–4 | 1–2–3–4 | ||

5. After alternating back and forth four times, the meter finally settles into a duple groove, and the musicians proceed to take their solos. **Musical selection**: Dave Brubeck, *Blue Rondo à la Turk* (1959), opening.

Credits: "Blue Rondo a la Turk" By Dave Brubeck. Performed By the Dave Brubeck Quartet. Used by Arrangement with Derry Music Company.

Lecture Six—Transcript
Meter, Part 2

This is Lecture Six and it is entitled "Meter, Part 2."

Metric Consistency

In what we call the music of the *Common Practice Period* (from roughly 1600–1900, spanning the Baroque, Classical, and Romantic Eras) the meter of a particular movement will tend to stay the same from the beginning to the end. Now, yes, there are exceptions, but for the most part, once a meter is established at the beginning of a movement, it will continue until the end of the movement. All such metric bets are off in the 20th and 21st centuries, during which changing meter—sometimes changing in every measure—becomes as common as changing pitch!

Syncopation

The most basic and common manner by which a composer can manipulate our sense of beat and meter is through a technique called *syncopation*. A syncopation is an accent where we do not expect an accent. Syncopation can take two forms: One, it can be an accent, or series, of unpatterned accents, used to create a sense of rhythmic interest, ambiguity, and/or tension. Two, a composer might employ a pattern of syncopations that, in effect, momentarily change the meter during a given passage of music! I'll demonstrate these two basic types of syncopation one at a time.

First, an accent, or series, of unpatterned accents used to create a sense of rhythmic interest, ambiguity, and/or tension. As our first example of such syncopation, we turn to the third movement of Beethoven's String Quartet in C Minor, op. 18, no. 4 of 1799. The movement is labeled as being a minuet and, as we would expect, it is set in triple meter. But, contrary to our expectations, Beethoven proceeds to accent—to almost obsessively accent—beat three instead of beat one. Question: Why the syncopations? Answer: to create conflict, ambiguity, and sheer musical excitement in what was for Beethoven an increasingly obsolescent musical genre—the minuet. Let's hear the opening of the movement, and I will count it. [**Musical example:** Ludwig van Beethoven, String Quartet no. 4 in C Minor, op. 18 (1799); movement 3, opening]

The musical genre of ragtime depends entirely on syncopation to create its characteristic sound. Ragtime is a piano music developed by African-American musicians at the end of the 19th century. Like the spiritual, blues, jazz, and rock & roll, ragtime is a composite music, a synthesis, a musical wedding of vastly different elements, some western European and some West African in origin. In the case of ragtime, the western European element is the marching band music that was so fabulously popular in the United States around the turn of the 20th century, of which the marches of John Philip Sousa are the preeminent examples. The West African element of ragtime is its rhythmic profile. You see, in ragtime, the complex poly- or multiple rhythmic layers of West African drumming are transferred to the piano, with a march-like, on-the-beat accompaniment supporting off-the-beat, syncopated music above.

Here's what we're going to do. We're going to listen to the opening of Scott Joplin's *Maple Leaf Rag* of 1899. Initially, we're just going to find and then clap to the beat, a rock-solid duple meter march beat. Once we've found the march groove—and it's about as tough to find as a woolly mammoth in your boudoir—I will ask you to continue clapping that march beat along with the pianist's left hand, while I scat sing the accents, the syncopations being played by the pianist's right hand. What we will discover is that those accents don't quite line up with the march beat; they will be either slightly ahead, or behind and the rhythmic tension created by these two different rhythmic layers is the essence of what ragtime is all about. It's also, my friends, the essence of what jazz is all about, although jazzers will not call that rhythmic tension ragging the beat, but, rather, swinging the beat.

Here we go: First let's find the beat, and then I'll sing the syncopations. [**Musical selection:** Scott Joplin, *Maple Leaf Rag* (1899), opening] Excellent! We observed that syncopation can take two forms. We've just demonstrated the first: an accent, or series, of unpatterned accents on moments other than the downbeat. The second form is a pattern of syncopations that, in effect, momentarily change the meter of a given passage of music! For example, let's say we're in triple meter. We expect an accent on one of every group of three. [**Demonstration of meter:** 1–2–3, 1–2–3, 1–2–3, 1–2–3] Now, let's say that for a number of consecutive measures, a composer accents every other beat instead of every third beat.

[**Demonstration of meter:** 1–2–3, 1–2–3, 1–2–3, 1–2–3, 1–2–3, 1–2–3, 1–2–3, 1–2–3] By syncopating every other beat, a composer will have, de facto, momentarily changed the meter from triple to duple, because we're hearing an accent every second, rather than every third beat. Again, let me count four measures of regular triple and then I will syncopate every other beat. [**Demonstration of meter:** 1–2–3, 1–2–3, 1–2–3, 1–2–3, 1–2–3, 1–2–3, 1–2, 1–2, 1–2, 1–2–3, 1–2–3, 1–2–3, 1–2–3]

Such a rhythmic event is called a *hemiola*, one of the nastiest sounding words in the musical lexicon: *hemiola*. A hemiola is a pattern of syncopations that creates the momentary impression of a change of meter, for example, the first theme of the first movement of Beethoven's Symphony no. 3, the *Eroica*. The movement is in triple meter, and so begins the opening theme, until about half-way through, when, suddenly, it goes rhythmically haywire, as a pattern of syncopations (a hemiola) momentarily appears to shift the meter to duple before correcting itself and shifting back to triple for the conclusion of the theme. I'll count it. You listen. [**Musical selection:** Ludwig van Beethoven, Symphony no, 3 in Eb Major, op. 55 (*Eroica*, 1803), movement 1, opening] This rhythmic ambiguity, this hemiola returns with a vengeance at the climactic moment of the movement, during which huge dissonances are pounded out in hemiolas. This is music of utter negation: Because of the dissonances, we sense no key area, and because of the hemiolas, we sense no consistent meter. This is as brutal as Beethoven's musical language will allow him to be and even today, this passage shocks. I'll count it. You listen. [**Musical selection:** Ludwig van Beethoven, Symphony no, 3 in Eb Major, op. 55 (*Eroica*, 1803), movement 1, development]

Beethoven was one of the most rhythmically inventive composers who ever lived, isolating and manipulating rhythm in a way that was unique in his time. I would suggest that one of the reasons why Beethoven's music remains so modern and edgy and viscerally powerful for us today is his rhythmic audacity, his manipulation of our sense of time, which is, frankly, very 21st century.

Compound Meter

A compound meter is any meter that features a triple subdivision within each beat. I will explain with a musical example. We're going to hear the fourth and final movement of Johannes Brahms' absolutely spectacular Trio for Violin, Piano, and Horn of 1865. Everything would seem to be moving by in groups of three, so, I will count the piece as if it were in triple meter. [**Musical selection:** Johannes Brahms, Trio for Violin, Piano, and Horn in Eb Major, op. 40 (1865), movement 4, opening] My friends, we have a problem here and I'm not just referring to my lips, which are presently in danger of combusting after having counted that music in three. Can any of us clap, or tap, our feet, or dance comfortably to the beats I just counted? I don't care how fast you are on your feet, whether you're Bill "Bojangles" Robinson, John Bubbles, Sammy Davis Jr., or Gregory Hines reincarnate, those beats grouped in threes are simply too fast to be considered the primary beats in this music.

So, we move up to the next rhythmic level. We hear each three-note grouping, or triplet, as constituting a single beat. Let's listen to that excerpt again and I'll clap that slower beat; feel free to clap along. [**Musical selection:** Johannes Brahms, Trio for Violin, Piano, and Horn in Eb Major, op. 40 (1865), movement 4, opening] Now, that's still pretty fast, but we can move to that beat, which is the primary beat and—low and behold!—that primary beat is being grouped in twos. [**Musical selection:** Johannes Brahms, Trio for Violin, Piano, and Horn in Eb Major, op. 40 (1865), movement 4, opening; Professor Greenberg counts the beats.] So, what have we got here? We have a meter in which the primary beats are subdivided into very fast groups of three. We call such a meter a compound meter because it is a composite of two different rhythmic levels: a primary beat that is subdivided into a fast group of three. This particular meter is called compound duple meter, because the primary beat is in duple. [**Demonstration of meter:** 1–2–3, 2–2–3, 1–2–3, 2–2–3, 1–2–3, 2–2–3, 1–2–3, 2–2–3] [**Musical selection:** Johannes Brahms, Trio for Violin, Piano, and Horn in Eb Major, op. 40 (1865), movement 4, opening; Professor Greenberg counts the beats.]

For another example of compound duple, we turn to the opening of the third and final movement of Bach's *Brandenburg* Concerto no. 6 in Bb Major, circa 1721. [**Demonstration of meter:** 1–2–3, 2–2–3, 1–2–3, 2–2–3, 1–2–3, 2–2–3, 1–2–3, 2–2–3] [**Musical selection:** Johann Sebastian Bach, *Brandenburg* Concerto no. 6 in Bb Major, BWV 1051 (c. 1721), movement 3, opening; Professor Greenberg counts the beats.] Compound duple meter is most usually notated as a time signature of six-over-eight (as what's called 6/8 time) meaning that there are two fast groups of three, or six eighth notes in every metric unit. Musicians know, when they see a time signature of 6/8, to beat the music in compound duple meter. One more example of compound duple meter: the first theme of the first movement of Beethoven's Symphony no. 7 of 1812. [**Musical selection:** Ludwig van Beethoven, Symphony no. 7 in A Major, op. 92 (1812), movement 1, theme 1; Professor Greenberg counts the beats.]

Now, there is also such a meter as compound triple, in which, again, each of the primary beats is subdivided into a fast group of three. As an example of compound triple meter, let's hear Johann Sebastian Bach's Two-Part Invention in G Major of 1723 and we'll count it this way. [**Demonstration of meter:** 1–2–3, 2–2–3, 3–2–3, 1–2–3, 2–2–3, 3–2–3] [**Musical selection:** Johann Sebastian Bach, Two-Part Invention no. 10 in G Major, BWV 781 (1723); Professor Greenberg counts the beats.]

There's an important point to be made regarding compound meter: Any meter perceived as being a compound meter will be, by definition, fast in tempo. Now, my friends, why should that be? Usually, tempo and meter have nothing to do with each other. Tempo refers to the speed of the beat, and the meter refers to how the beats are grouped, which are two entirely different things. It's true, except when it comes to compound meter. Let's go back to the Bach Invention in G Major, set in compound triple meter. Now, as you recall, it began this way. [**Piano example:** Johann Sebastian Bach, Two-Part Invention no. 10 in G Major, BWV 781 (1723), measures 1–2] We perceive this as compound meter because the triplet subdivisions of the beat are too fast to feel as the primary beats. But, what would happen if we slowed this music down more and more? [**Piano example:** Johann Sebastian Bach, Two-Part Invention no. 10 in G Major, BWV 781 (1723), opening, played slower and slower and finally played in slow waltz time] Well, sooner or later, my friends, we'll cross a threshold: sooner or later, those formerly fast subdivisions of three will begin to feel like the primary beats and that's why I did that terrible thing and turned the end of that last excerpt into a waltz. If we go slowly enough, one measure of compound triple meter will eventually sound like three measures of regular triple meter. Thus, for us to properly perceive a meter as being compound, the tempo must be fast enough that the triplet subdivisions will be perceived as subdivisions, and not as the primary beats.

Conversely, let's say a composer notates a movement in triple meter, assigning a time signature of three-quarter time and, then, that same composer turns around and marks the movement *molto vivace* (very lively—meaning "very fast"), just as Beethoven does in the second movement of his Symphony no. 9 of 1824. [**Musical selection:** Ludwig van Beethoven, Symphony no. 9 in D Minor, op. 125 (1824) movement 2, opening] Does this sound like triple meter? Well, according to the notated time signature it is. But, as listeners, we do not perceive it as being triple meter. At this tempo, the individual beats are simply too fast to consider as being the primary beat and I would tell you that conductors do not conduct this movement in three, but, rather, in one. There is no term for a meter like this; for our information, there is no such term as compound single. We'll just have to stick with triple meter that's so fast that we feel it and conduct it in one, and leave it at that!

Additive Meter

By this point of our three-lecture survey of beat and meter, we should be feeling fairly confident about our ability to identify duple and triple meter. So, in the spirit of "let's identify one more," I present to you the second movement of Tchaikovsky's Symphony no. 6 of 1893. My friends, find the beat, feel around for accentuation, and determine whether the beats are groupings of two, or three. [**Musical selection:** Peter Ilyich Tchaikovsky, Symphony no. 6 in B Minor, op. 74 (1893), movement 2, opening] Hmm. That music's got the lilt and feel of a waltz, yes? So it must be in triple meter, yes? So let's count it in three. [**Musical selection:** Peter Ilyich Tchaikovsky, Symphony no. 6 in B Minor, op. 74 (1893), movement 2, opening] Now that didn't work at all. Is it a compound meter, you ask? No. Is it filled with syncopations and hemiolas? No. Then, what the heck is going on? It's an additive meter, which is some combination of twos and threes. As it is, the meter of Tchaikovsky's movement is a five, arrayed as a three plus a two. Count with me. [**Musical selection:** Peter Ilyich Tchaikovsky, Symphony no. 6 in B Minor, op. 74 (1893), movement 2, opening] Now doesn't that feel better! No wonder the movement has been referred to as "the Five-Legged Waltz." It sounds like a waltz, it feels like a waltz, but it's missing a beat every other measure! Hey, who says Pete Tchaikovsky didn't have a sense of humor! While additive meter is common in any number of eastern European folk traditions, until the 20th century, it was very rarely used in western European music. What this means is that when we do hear additive meter in pre-20th century concert music, it will almost always be in works by eastern European composers, like Tchaikovsky.

Another example: Modest Mussorgsky begins his magnificent *Pictures at an Exhibition* of 1874 with a movement entitled "Promenade." The "Promenade" begins with a fanfare that consists of four metric units of 11 beats each, spelled out in the score as a five plus a six. Let's listen to this opening and let's count to 11 four times! [**Musical selection:** Modest Mussorgsky, *Pictures at an Exhibition* (1874), "Promenade," opening] The "Promenade" music we just heard returns periodically, representing, as it does, our promenade, our stroll through an exhibition of drawings, designs, sketches, and water colors by Mussorgsky's friend, the architect Victor Alexandrovich Hartmann. In an appearance about halfway through the piece, the additive meter that characterized the opening of the first "Promenade" goes into hyperdrive, as Mussorgsky mixes and matches a whole bunch of different meters. Here's what happens: This "Promenade," like the first one, begins with four units of 11, each spelled out as a five plus a six. Then there are two units of six, followed by an 11, a six, another 11, two sixes, then two sevens, and finally, three more 11s. You got that? $11 + 11 + 11 + 11 + 6 + 6 + 11 + 6 + 11 + 6 + 6 + 7 + 7 + 11 + 11 + 11$. I'll count; you listen. [**Musical selection:** Modest Mussorgsky, *Pictures at an Exhibition* (1874), "Promenade"]

Sidebar—Metric Asymmetry

Mussorgsky indicates that the "Promenade" movements in *Pictures at an Exhibition*, including the one we just heard, be played *allegro giusto, nel modo russico*, which means "moderately fast and in Russian style." We ask, rightly: What does Mussorgsky mean by "Russian style?" It's the rhythm, my friends, the additive meters as well as the rhythmic asymmetry created by all the different meters. It's a sort of asymmetry that's characteristic of the Russian language and Russian folk music and it's a sort of rhythmic asymmetry that the Russian-born Igor Stravinsky will cultivate to extremes during the course of his long career. We turn, as an example, to Igor Stravinsky's *The Rite of Spring* of 1912 for a perfect example of metric asymmetry gone wild! At the conclusion of an episode called "The Game of the Abduction," we hear this dizzying succession of different meters: $3 + 5 + 5 + 3 + 4 + 5 + 6 + 5 + 2 + 6 + 6 + 6 + 6 + 2 + 6 + 4 + 6 + 6 + 4 + 6 + 6 + 6 + 4 + 2$. Let's hear it. [**Musical selection:** Igor Stravinsky, *The Rite of Spring* (1912), "The Game of the Abduction"] I know you want to hear that again. So, let's hear that again! [**Musical selection:** Igor Stravinsky, *The Rite of Spring* (1912), "The Game of the Abduction"] This is incredibly exciting music, in which the excitement is almost entirely a function of the unpredictable nature of its metric asymmetry!

Back to Additive Meter

Now please, let's not confuse additive meter with metric asymmetry. A passage of music characterized by metric asymmetry—as we just observed in Stravinsky's *The Rite of Spring*—exhibits no particular repeated metric pattern. As opposed to additive meter, which is just another sort of patterned meter, like duple and triple, an additive meter is one made up of some combination of twos and threes. As we observed earlier, in the 19th century, additive meter—on those rare occasions when it was used at all—was generally the province of eastern European composers. Having said that, all bets are off when it comes to the 20th and 21st centuries, during which additive and asymmetrical meter became part of the common syntax of Western music.

Of all the experiments with additive meter in the music of the twentieth century, no composers dedicated more of their creative energies to creating a body of music employing additive meter than did the pianist Dave Brubeck and the alto saxophonist Paul Desmond. An easy confession, my friends. Growing up, I worshipped the Dave Brubeck Quartet, in both of its permutations: its first permutation, with Paul Desmond on alto sax, and in its second, with Gerry Mulligan on baritone sax. Brubeck himself has always been, for me, a musical hero, a first rate pianist and a superb composer, who has created what I believe will be a lasting body of first-rate work, from his jazz numbers and songs to his concert works and oratorios. I had the privilege of participating in a performance of Brubeck's oratorio, *The Gates of Justice*, when I was in high school in 1971 and it was a life-altering experience for me. And I will tell you that never will you meet a nicer, more generous, more good-spirited man than Dave Brubeck.

Anyway, Brubeck and his quartet recorded five "concept" albums between 1959 and 1966. Entitled *Time Out, Time Further Out, Time Changes, Countdown: Time in Outer Space*, and *Time In*, the avowed mission of these albums was to "break the tyranny of duple meter" and create a body of jazz in triple meter, additive meter, and multiple simultaneous meters. The most famous individual piece from this period of metric experimentation is *Take Five*, written by Paul Desmond. As I'm sure you've already guessed, if you didn't already know, *Take Five* is in five, with the beats arrayed as a three plus two: 1–2–3, 1–2, 1–2–3, 1–2, 1–2–3, 1–2 and so forth. The movie and television composer Lalo Schifrin took a page from Desmond's *Take Five* when he composed his *Mission Impossible* theme in 1966, which is also in five and also breaks down to a three-plus-two [**Demonstration of meter:** 1–2–3, 1–2, 1–2–3, 1–2, 1–2–3, 1–2, 1–2–3, 1–2] We're going to conclude this lecture with a piece by Dave Brubeck, the rather painfully titled *Blue Rondo à la Turk* of 1959. The piece is neither a rondo, nor terribly "blue" (as in "blues-like"), though Brubeck claims that the additive rhythms he employs were inspired by folk music he heard on tour in Turkey. Whatever, it's a great piece, and here's how it works. The theme itself is set in nine, which is subdivided in two different ways. The first subdivision of those nine beats is: 1–2, 1–2, 1–2, 1–2–3, 1–2, 1–2, 1–2, 1–2–3. All right. What have we got here? Three sets of two and one set of three, all of which adds up to nine: 1–2, 1–2, 1–2, 1–2–3. Say it with me three times in succession. Ready? Here we go: 1–2, 1–2, 1–2, 1–2–3 [repeated three times]. Excellent. I'll play the first three measures of the piece, slowly and we'll hear how the subdivisions of 1–2, 1–2, 1–2, 1–2–3 lay out in those measures. [**Piano example:** Dave Brubeck, *Blue Rondo à la Turk* (1959), measures 1–3; as he plays, Professor Greenberg counts the beats.] And now the interesting part. Every fourth measure, every fourth metric unit, Brubeck changes the way he subdivides the nine beats, going from: 1–2, 1–2, 1–2, 1–2–3 to 1–2–3, 1–2–3, 1–2–3. So here's the metric pattern that will repeat itself every four measures: 1–2, 1–2, 1–2, 1–2–3 [repeated three times]. 1–2–3, 1–2–3, 1–2–3. Let's all do that together: 1–2, 1–2, 1–2, 1–2–3 [repeated three times] 1–2–3, 1–2–3, 1–2–3. [**Musical selection:** Dave Brubeck, *Blue Rondo à la Turk* (1959), opening]

Now, I would point out the tempo of this piece is rather fast and as such, Brubeck's subdivisions can also be felt at a higher rhythmic level: The groups of two can be felt as a single, short beat and the groups of three as a single, long beat. Let me show you what I mean and I'm going to clap on the ones. [**Demonstration of meter:** Professor Greenbergs claps on the first beat while he counts the beats: 1–2, 1–2, 1–2, 1–2–3 (repeated three times), 1–2–3, 1–2–3, 1–2–3. Short–short–short–long (repeated three times), long–long–long]

However we choose to count it, Brubeck is saving his best rhythmic trick for last. One minute and 52 seconds into the recording, the music begins alternating back and forth between 1–2, 1–2, 1–2, 1–2–3, 1–2, 1–2, 1–2, 1–2–3 and straight, swinging duple meter, in which the beats are the same length as the long 1–2–3. Here's what it will sound like. [**Demonstration of meter:** Professor Greenberg claps on the first beats while he counts the beats: 1–2, 1–2, 1–2, 1–2–3 (repeated three times), 1–2–3, 1–2–3, 1–2–3, 1–2–3–4, 1–2–3–4] After alternating back and forth four times, the meter finally settles into the jazzy, duple groove and the musicians proceed to take their solos. Let's listen from the beginning. At first, I'll count the fast beats, 1–2, 1–2, 1–2, 1–2–3, 1–2, 1–2, 1–2, 1–2–3 and so forth. Then, I'll identify the larger beats by speaking "short–short–short–long." Then, I'll zip it until the meter begins to alternate between additive and duple, at which time, I'll start counting again. Here we go! [**Musical selection:** Dave Brubeck, *Blue Rondo à la Turk* (1959), opening]

Concluding Review

The smallest time division in a given section of music to which we can comfortably move our bodies is called the beat, or pulse. The speed at which the beat, or pulse moves is called the tempo. Most music—certainly the overwhelming majority of music composed between 1600 and 1900—will exhibit a pattern of accentuation that will allow the listener to identify patterns of beats called meter. Meter refers to how beats are grouped in a given section of music. Thank you!

Lecture Seven
Pitch and Mode, Part 1

Scope:
A given sound, the product of a concussion wave, may be perceived as noise or as a discrete sound that features a single fundamental frequency, one that we can comfortably sing. A *pitch* is a discrete sound characterized by a fundamental frequency with the attribute of timbre. A *note* is a pitch that has been notated and, thus, has been given duration. The modern Western orchestra is tuned to concert A. This has a fundamental frequency of 440 cycles per second. Although different cultures employ different pitch collections in their music, Western music currently uses a 12-pitch collection.

Outline

I. Our discussion of pitch begins with an exploration of the nature of sound.

   A. What we perceive as sound is the product of a concussion wave: tiny changes in air pressure.

      1. The depression of the key that plays the pitch C on a piano begins a process that will make the piano's soundboard vibrate. **Piano example**.

      2. Air molecules oscillate in sympathy with the vibrating soundboard, sending out a concussion wave as the air pressure fluctuates.

      3. The concussion wave causes the thin membrane of the eardrum to vibrate, starting a process in which the vibrations are eventually converted into electric impulses that our brains interpret as a specific sound coming from a specific direction.

   B. In musical terms, *noise* can be defined as too much sonic information for the brain to interpret as a singable pitch.

      1. A single piano key, when depressed, produces a discrete pitch. **Piano examples**: pitch of C and C-major chord.

      2. There is a threshold past which our ear cannot single out individual discrete pitches. **Piano example**: cluster of pitches (noise).

3. The most extreme example of noise is white noise or static: a sound made up of all or nearly all audible sounds.

4. Non-pitched percussion instruments produce "noise" sounds that, unlike white noise, have attributes of timbre and register. We can tell the difference between a drum and a cymbal, for example. **Musical selection**: Robert Greenberg, *It Don't Mean a Thing* (1989).

II. Some sounds exhibit a single fundamental frequency, a discrete sound, one that we can comfortably sing.

A. When, for example, piano strings vibrate, the most important vibration is on the string's full length. **Piano example**: concert A plucked on piano string.

1. If our piano is in tune, the just-plucked string will vibrate back and forth on its full length 440 times a second. In other words, that string's fundamental frequency is 440 times per second. **Piano example**: concert A.

2. When we hear a sound we can sing, we are singing along with the discrete sound's fundamental frequency. **Piano example**: concert A.

B. A *pitch* is a discrete sound characterized by a fundamental frequency with the attribute of timbre.

1. When piano strings vibrate, they produce secondary vibrations that give off sounds that are higher than the fundamental frequency because they are produced by smaller increments of the string.

2. These higher sounds are called *overtones* or *harmonics*, and their number and intensity goes a long way to determining the timbre of a given instrument (or voice). **Piano example**: pitch of concert A.

3. The timbre of that A will vary tremendously depending on what instrument is playing it. The timbral difference is largely a product of an instrument's overtone signature, which is, in turn, a product of the size of the instrument, what it is made of, how it is played, and numerous other variables.

C. A note is a discrete sound with the attributes of timbre and duration. A note is a pitch that has been notated.

1. Pitches are notated on a five-line graph (*staff*). The higher the note head representing the pitch is placed on the staff, the higher it sounds.
2. The duration of such pitches (how long they are held, or sustained) is indicated by hollow note heads or solid note heads and by adding various stems and flags to the note head.
3. The general rule of thumb is that the more "stuff" attached to a note, the shorter its duration.
4. It is incorrect to say, "I am going to play a *note* on the piano," unless that pitch has been notated and given duration.

D. The A above middle C is a very special pitch called concert A. This is the pitch to which Western orchestral players tune their instruments before a performance.
1. By the early 19th century, concert A hovered around a fundamental frequency of 430. Modern instruments are tuned to A = 440.
2. The difference between these frequencies is discernable in the following comparison. **Musical selection**: Ludwig van Beethoven, Symphony no. 3 in Eb Major, op. 55 (1803), movement 1, opening (period instruments pitched at A = 430; same piece of music repeated with a modern orchestra pitched at A = 440).
3. In 1885, an international conference in Vienna recommended universal adoption of an 1859 French recommendation that A should be pitched at a fundamental frequency of 435 cycles per second.
4. This remained the most widely used pitch standard until the universal adoption of A = 440 in the 20th century.

E. Western pitch collections of the last 400 years represent a balance between melody and harmony: a reconciliation of melodic structures and harmonic structures based on the overtone series.
1. Since approximately 1600, Western music has overwhelmingly relied on three particular pitch collections: major, minor, and chromatic.
2. The term *melody* describes any succession of pitches.

3. The term *harmony* describes the sound and relationship between pitches heard simultaneously.
4. The term *scale* implies a stepwise ordering of pitches, climbing up or down. As such, the term *scale* cannot be properly used to address a group of pitches in which no ordering is implied. The proper term to describe a group of pitches arrayed around a single tonal center (or tonic pitch) is *collection*.

F. Different cultures have invented and employed different pitch collections.
1. Traditional Japanese music uses a 5-pitch collection.
2. Western music currently uses a 12-pitch collection.
3. Some Arab music uses a 17-pitch collection.
4. The American composer Harry Partch created a 43-pitch collection.
5. What all these pitch collections have in common is the primacy of the interval of the octave.

G. An *interval* is the relationship between any two pitches.
1. The interval of an octave is acknowledged as the essential building block of any pitch system. **Piano examples**: two Cs an octave apart, demonstrating consonance (repeated); C and Db, demonstrating dissonance.
2. The ancient Greek philosopher and arithmetician Pythagoras experimented with numerical ratios in relation to sound. When he plucked a string, he discovered that the 1:1 ratio produces a unison and, therefore, consonant sound. **Piano example**: low C (repeated).
3. When he divided the same string in half, the plucked sound—a 2:1 ratio—produces a consonant sound. **Piano examples**: low C and C one octave higher.
4. Pythagoras realized that the simpler the numerical ratios between vibrating bodies, the more blended and consonant the sounds created by those vibrating bodies.
5. Pythagoras's discovery had profound meaning for him and his fellow Greeks, who came to view music as the sonic manifestation of cosmic order.

Lecture Seven—Transcript
Pitch and Mode, Part 1

This is Lecture Seven and it is entitled "Pitch and Mode, Part 1." Music is sound in time, or time defined by sound. Having spent the previous three lectures talking about the time aspect of music, it's time, now, to return to the sound aspect of music. I will confess to you, up front, that I've spent a lot of my own time trying to decide in exactly what order to present the next seven lectures worth of material. I'm a firm believer that good teaching is good story-telling and that every good story has a beginning, middle, and end; a lead story as well as a back story, or two; maybe a little romantic interest; a surprise along the way; after which, C major gets the girl and all the keys and modes, both major and minor, live happily ever after.

Having acknowledged that this is how I'd like to be able to tell the story of pitch, I must confess that this story, which includes the historical development of pitch collections (also known as scales), intervals, mode, melody, texture, the concepts of consonance and dissonance, and the overtone series, yes, this story is a most challenging one to tell in a coherent, linear fashion. For example, to understand pitch collections (or scales), we must first understand something of the overtone series, but, to understand the importance of the overtone series in the development of tonality, we must first know something about the historical development of musical texture, and to understand texture, we've got to know something about the nature of melody, but, to understand melody we've got to know something about pitch collections, and now look, I've gone and confused myself. The point: as we move forward and encounter new information and master various listening skills, it will be necessary to occasionally digress, criss-cross, respeak and rethink previously covered material in the light of new material. I know you're with me for the long haul so, by the time we put a wrap on this course, everything should be in its proper place. Onward!

Sound

We are going to examine the actual sounds of music hierarchically, from the most general to the specific. Thus, we must begin by defining sound itself. When we ask the average person, What is sound? The answer we're most likely to receive is that sound is a wave—sound waves, right? Immediately we conjure up in our mind's eye waves and rays and beams of sound cresting and shooting about all around us. Incorrecto. In reality, what we perceive as sound is the product of a concussion wave, the subtle jostling of air molecules responding to tiny changes in air pressure that we perceive as sound. Let's check out the process. I'm going to press a key on the piano. That downward pressure is going to lever a felt-covered hammer upwards, where it will strike a string, setting that string in motion. That string will begin to vibrate in all sorts of complex patterns (which we'll discuss in due time). The vibrating string is, at the far end of the piano, in contact with a bridge, which itself is connected to the sound board of the piano. The vibrating string induces the bridge to vibrate and the bridge transmits those vibrations to the soundboard of the piano, which will, as a result, also begin to vibrate. [**Piano example:** C] I trust we all heard that sound. We heard it, because the air molecules up against the soundboard of the piano began to move back and forth in sympathy with the vibrating soundboard. Like dominoes falling outwards from a central source, the gazillions of molecules that make up the air in The Teaching Company studio bumped one into the next, sending out a concussion wave, as the air pressure fluctuated. It all happens very quickly, my friends. The speed of sound at sea level is around 1150 feet per second, so, if you're five feet away from the piano, the concussion wave (the fluctuation in air pressure) takes less than a two-hundredth of a second to reach your ears, or, as the case may be, the diaphragm of the microphones recording the sound. But, for now, let's just assume that you're in the studio with me.

Let's contemplate for a moment our ears, nature's own radar dishes, which gather and focus the concussion wave. We hear binaurally; that is, we've got two ears (unless, of course, you're Vincent van Gogh), one on either side of our heads (unless, of course, you're a painting by Picasso), an arrangement that allows for directional hearing. You see, since the fluctuation in air pressure that is the concussion wave will reach the ear closer to the source of the sound a tiny bit of time before it reaches the other ear, we're wired to interpret that differential as directional and we can therefore locate the source of the sound, of the concussion wave, of the fluctuation in air pressure, almost instantly. Oh, it's most remarkable. But, we get ahead of ourselves!

The concussion wave (the fluctuation in air pressure) induces that incredibly thin membrane that is our eardrum to vibrate. The vibrating eardrum, in turn, induces the three tiny bones in our middle ears—the hammer, the anvil, and the stirrup bone—to vibrate. These bones, collectively called our ossicles, induce the viscous fluid in our inner ears to slosh back and forth which causes the basilar membrane (which is one of the membranes that divides our inner ear in half) to vibrate, vibrations that are eventually converted into electric impulses, which our brains interpret as the sound of a piano coming from over there.

And please, that's just a single sound. For a moment, let's contemplate the miracle of our hearing: Imagine the seemingly infinite complexity of the concussion waves our ears are assaulted by when listening to an 85-piece orchestra in a symphony hall, with each instrument contributing its own unique sonic signature to the morass of jiggling air molecules in the hall. Some of the concussion waves are received directly from the orchestra, while others arrive at various later increments of time, having been reflected, as they are, off the sides, rear, floor, and ceiling of the hall. Even as our eardrums are being battered by this almost infinitely complex amount of vibration, we are simultaneously aware of the idiot behind us crinkling her lozenge wrapper, and the moron next to us tapping his program against his knee, and the consumptive cretin somewhere in the back of the theater hacking away like the Marlboro Man in a sandstorm, and the pinheaded imbecile somewhere in front of us trying to turn off the ringer of her cell phone. Somehow, through the interactive miracle of our ears and our brains, we interpret and understand this tangle of fluctuating air pressure as representing the individual instrumental voices that are collectively an orchestra, to say nothing of the various unwelcome noises created by the nitwits around us. If we wanted to, we could even look over at that really cute flute player sitting halfway back on stage and isolate her sound from the rest. No wonder my grandmother told me "never put anything in your ears smaller than a breadbox" (a Q-tip being the exception). Who wants to mess with such a delicate and extraordinary bit of apparatus! And let's not forget, my friends, that there are creatures whose hearing leaves ours in the dust: dogs, cats, owls, whales, and bats to name but a few. Anyway, it's all amazing. Sound—and its most perfect manifestation, music—is the very vibration of the world around us. Let's begin our investigation of sound by exploring the different sorts of sounds.

Noise

We begin with what is, perhaps, the most general classification of sound, that being noise. Noise is one of those words that has an armful of colloquial meanings, but, as a musical term, just one meaning. Be forewarned, I'm going to smack my music stand. [**Demonstration:** Professor Greenberg smacks the stand.] Can we sing that sound? No, we can't. My friends, smack something nearby, go ahead, only make sure that the object you smack is inanimate! (And no, your husband or teenage son does not qualify, motionless and seemingly comatose though he may be.) Can you sing the sound your smack produced? No, you can't and the reason why you can't is that the impact of your hand, on whatever object you struck, produced so much sonic information that you simply cannot single out any particular pitch to sing.

Let's approach this issue of noise, this issue of too much sonic information from another angle. For reasons we'll talk about in just a moment, when I press a single key on the piano, what's produced is something called a single discrete pitch: a single, discrete sound that we can single out, identify, and sing. [**Piano example:** Professor Greenberg sings and plays the pitch of C] We should all be able to sing that pitch. Now, I can press multiple different keys simultaneously and, providing I don't press too many at the same time, we can still make out individual discrete pitches and we can still sing them. [**Piano example:** Professor Greenberg plays a C-major chord and sings the component pitches] However my friends, there's a threshold past which our ears simply cannot single out individual discrete pitches, a threshold at which we perceive, instead, an indistinguishable mass of indistinguishable sound. [**Piano example**]

That's noise. Properly and non-subjectively defined, noise is the presence of so much sonic information that we cannot distinguish individual pitched sounds and as a result, we perceive instead the mass of sound itself. The most extreme example of noise would be so-called white noise, or static. Just as what we perceive as white is the simultaneous presence of all light spectra, so what we call white noise is a sound made up of all or nearly all audible sounds.

©2007 The Teaching Company

Excepting experimental electronic music and middle school orchestras, we will generally not hear white noise used in a musical context.

Noise Instruments—Percussion

Obviously, not all noise is white noise. Non-pitched percussion instruments, for example, produce sounds that are noise sounds. My friends, we cannot sing the sound of a snare drum, though such sounds, unlike white noise, have the attributes of timbre and register. We can, after all, tell the difference between a drum and a cymbal, a timbral difference, and between high, medium, and low drums, a registral difference, for example. As an example of various percussion instruments, I humbly offer an excerpt of a percussion piece of my own composition entitled *It Don't Mean a Thing* for six percussionists playing about 40 percussion instruments of various types, from timpani and a variety of drums and cymbals to wood blocks, temple blocks, and brake drums. A brake drum, my friends, is just what it sounds like it is: the round metal collar from a truck or automobile wheel on which the brake shoe rubs in order to stop a vehicle. Brake drums produce a brilliant, ringing, metallic sound when struck with a hard mallet and, the bigger the brake drum, the lower its sound. For percussionists, the world is their instrument, and there's nothing percussionists enjoy more than a trip to the junkyard in search of stuff they can hit! Anyway, we're going to hear the closing minutes of the piece, frankly, more than enough to demonstrate that a large percussion ensemble can sound, in its own way, quite orchestral in its variety of timbres and registers. *It Don't Mean a Thing* of 1989. [**Musical selection:** Robert Greenberg, *It Don't Mean a Thing* (1989)]

Some noise sounds are really good and we gain, I think, new insight into the vast and often pleasing variety of sounds that constitute noise if we avoid using the word subjectively, as opposed to, yes, my dictionary. It's been a while since I quoted my Webster's Collegiate and I feel, at this moment, compelled to do so, as its definition of noise is so subjective as to be genuinely comic: "Noise: a loud, confused, or senseless outcry; a sound that lacks agreeable musical quality or is noticeably loud, harsh, or discordant." [Webster's Seventh New Collegiate Dictionary, 572] It's hard to imagine a more subjective definition. One wonders if the person who coined that definition—perhaps Mr. Webster himself—was living next door to a punk band that practiced in their garage, or, perhaps, a student bagpipe player? Onward, please to pitched sounds!

Fundamental Frequency

Some sounds exhibit a single fundamental frequency, what is called a discrete sound. Put another way, a discrete sound, that is, a sound we can comfortably sing, is characterized by a fundamental frequency. I explain. When certain sorts of objects vibrate—a violin or piano string, for example—they wiggle and wobble in all sorts of ways, something we'll discuss when we get to the overtone series. Having said that, the most important wobble is the one on the string's full length. For example, this piano string is about 19 inches long. [**Piano example:** pitch of concert A plucked on the piano string] If the piano is in tune, which it is, then when I press the appropriate key to strike that string [**Piano example:** concert A], that string will vibrate back-and-forth on its full length 440 times a second. We would say then that that string's fundamental frequency (how frequently it vibrates back-and-forth on its full length when struck, or plucked, or bowed) is 440 times a second. When we hear a sound with which we can sing along (meaning a discrete sound), what we are singing along with is its fundamental frequency, that vibration occurring along the full length of whatever object is vibrating. [**Piano example:** concert A] Sing that sound. When you sing that sound, your vocal chords, square inside your larynx, are also vibrating, on their full length, 440 times a second, unless you're singing out of tune which, for students of mine is, frankly, not a possibility. So, to review: Any sound we can sing (a discrete sound) will by definition be characterized by a clear and audible fundamental frequency, as it is that fundamental frequency that we sing.

Pitch

A *pitch* is a discrete sound, that is, a sound characterized by a fundamental frequency, with the attribute of timbre. I repeat: a pitch is a discrete sound, that is, a sound characterized by a fundamental frequency, with the attribute of timbre. I explain. When we look inside a piano, while it's being played, what we see are the hammers and dampers moving up and down. What we don't see are the strings actually vibrating; the movements are too small and subtle. But, if viewed under a stroboscope, what we see is amazing: The strings are not just wobbling and wiggling, they're actually dancing, with a precision that would put the Rockettes to shame! Aside from vibrating back and forth at its full length, a given string is also simultaneously vibrating back-and-forth at exactly half of its length, and at a third its length, and at a quarter, fifth, and sixth of its length, and so forth. These secondary vibrations also give off sounds, sounds that are higher than the fundamental frequency, which makes sense, as they are produced by smaller increments of the string. These higher sounds given off by the secondary vibrations are called overtones, or harmonics, and the number and intensity of these overtones goes a long way towards determining the timbre of a given instrument (or voice, for that matter). Hey, every pitched instrument in the orchestra can play an A. [**Piano example:** concert A] But, that's an A on a piano. Clearly, the timbre of that A will vary tremendously depending upon what instrument is playing it. That timbral difference is largely a product of an instrument's overtone signature, which is, in turn, a product of the size of the instrument, what it's made of, and how it's played, and a thousand-and-one other variables. So, back to our definition of pitch: A pitch is a discrete sound with the attribute of timbre, meaning, a pitch is a discrete sound played by an instrument or sung by a voice.

Note

A note is a discrete sound, that is, a sound characterized by a fundamental frequency, with the attributes of timbre and duration. In other words, a note is a pitch that can be notated, one that is sustained for a certain specified amount of time. Thus far in the course, the only elements of notation we've discussed are tempo markings, dynamic markings, bar lines and time signatures and while these are indeed important notational elements, they are not the primary elements of music notation. The primary elements of music notation are those that indicate sounds in time, meaning pitch and duration. In brief, my friends: Pitches are notated on a five-line graph, called a *staff*. The higher the note head representing a pitch is placed on the staff, the higher it sounds. The duration of such pitches, that is, for how long they are sustained, is indicated by using hollow note heads, or solid note heads, and by adding various stems to the note head and flags to the stems. A general rule-of-thumb regarding duration: The more stuff attached to a note, the shorter its duration. Back, please, to our definition of *note*.

It is incorrect then, to say, "I'm going to play a *note* on the piano" unless that pitch has a given duration. Now, look, I know this sounds like quibbling, but these are the sorts of words and distinctions that separate the informed from the un-informed. When I'm listening to a pre-concert talk and the speaker does not distinguish between *pitch* and *note*, I get annoyed and twitchy and turn to my wife and ask her why I should believe that this person knows anything about 19th-century French music if he can't properly distinguish between *pitch* and *note*, at which point my wife will tell me to chill and zip because she, at least, is listening, but you get my point. There are some words out there, that when mispronounced and/or misused, call into question entirely the knowledge, even the professionalism of the speaker. How about the "real-tor" who insists on calling herself a "real-a-tor"? (Oh, we once interviewed a "real-tor" who not only kept referring to herself as a "real-a-tor," but also referred to houses that hadn't sold after a certain period of time as having an "astigmatism" attached to them, rather than having a *stigma* attached to them. An "astigmatism," my friends. We did not hire that "real-tor.") On those same lines, I just love it when a jeweler says "jew-le-ry" instead of "jewel-ry," when, during a sports show, I love it when someone says "ath-e-lete" instead of "ath-lete," and when, while listening to a pain-relief medication ad, someone says "athur-i-tis" instead of "arthritis" and let's not even talk about world leaders who say "nu-cu-lar" instead of "nu-clear"; to mispronounce that word is just a bit scary. Where were we? Ah, yes, *note*. A *note*, then, is a notated pitch: a discrete sound with the attributes of timbre and duration.

Sidebar—Concert A, or A 440

The A above middle C on which we focused our explanation of pitch is, indeed, a very special pitch called concert A. It is the pitch to which the instruments of the orchestra tune immediately before a performance. Well, who decided that? It's a good question, one that has been the subject of books and dissertations. We will be rather more brief in our answer. My friends, it's a matter of anarchy versus order. Under the heading of anarchy, I would tell you that the earliest surviving manual on how to tune harpsichords, dating from 1523, suggests that the starting pitch, a C from which the other pitches could be tuned, could be placed as high, or as low, as one wished. Pitch anarchy! Sonic chaos! Yes, indeed, according to The New Grove Dictionary of Music and Musicians: "The concept of a precise and universal relation between notation and [actual] pitch was alien to most Western musicians [until] the eighteenth century." [The New Grove Dictionary of Music and Musicians, volume 14, 779].

By Beethoven's day (the early 19th century), concert A (the pitch to which the orchestra tuned) was lower than it is today; it hovered around a fundamental frequency of 430. The difference between A 430 and A 440 might sound slight, but it's immediately apparent if we compare performances of the same piece, one played by period instruments tuned to about A 430 and the other played by modern instruments tuned to A 440. A back-to-back comparison: Beethoven's Symphony no. 3 of 1803, played first by a period orchestra conducted by our good buddy, Conductor B followed immediately by a modern orchestra, conducted, rather slowly, if you recall, by our rather lugubrious friend, Conductor A. Note that the pitch will be noticeably higher in the second, modern orchestra version. First, the period instrument recording, in which A equals about 430. [**Musical selection:** Ludwig van Beethoven, Symphony no. 3 in Eb Major, op. 55 (1803), movement 1, opening] And now, a modern orchestra pitched at A 440. [**Musical selection:** Ludwig van Beethoven, Symphony no. 3 in Eb Major, op. 55 (1803), movement 1, opening] Let's hear that back-to-back one more time. Again, A equals about 430 [**Musical selection:** Ludwig van Beethoven, Symphony no. 3 in Eb Major, op. 55 (1803), movement 1, opening] and now a modern orchestra pitched at A equals 440 [**Musical selection:** Ludwig van Beethoven, Symphony no. 3 in Eb Major, op. 55 (1803), movement 1, opening]

The growing orchestras and larger performance venues of the 19th century demanded bigger and more sonorous stringed instruments, an impulse that led to the invention of the metal-harped piano as well. These larger stringed instruments were capable of supporting greater string tension and the strings—increasingly made from steel as opposed to gut—were tightened and the pitch raised in order to make the instruments more piercing and more brilliant. It was during the mid-19th century, when industrial technology began being applied to instrument construction, that absolute pitch standards came into being. In 1859, a French government commission recommended that A should be pitched at a fundamental frequency of 435 cycles per second. In 1885, an international conference in Vienna urged the universal adoption of this "French standard," and it remained the most widely used such pitch standard until the universal adoption of A equals 440 in the 20th century.

Sidebar, Continued—Perfect Pitch

A person who has *perfect pitch* is someone who, through some combination of genetic predisposition and early environmental exposure has memorized, at a primal level, A equals 440, and as a result can identify, instantly, any pitch she hears: "Oh, that's an F#; yes, that's a D; hm-mm, that's a B-natural." Wow, we think, we wish we could do that! We should be careful what we wish for. Having perfect pitch is great for parlor tricks, but a disaster if you're listening to any music that's not tuned to A 440, like a period performance pitched at A equals 430, or, much worse, any performance that's slightly out of tune. That will make the person with perfect pitch squirm in agony, just as the sentence "a 'real-a-tor' wearing 'jew-le-ry' told me that the 'nu-cu-lar' waste dump nearby gives this house an 'astigmatism,' like an 'ath-e-lete' with 'artur-i-tis'" will make me squirm in agony. Sidebar over!

Pitch Collections

Precisely what pitches to employ and how those pitches relate to one another is a basic aspect of any musical language. We will find that the Western pitch collections of the last 400 years represent a balance between melody and harmony: a reconciliation of melodic structures and harmonic structures based on the overtone series. That was quite a mouthful and I want to repeat it before we begin our exploration of pitch collections: We will find that the Western pitch collections of the last 400 years represent a balance between melody and harmony, a reconciliation of melodic structures and harmonic structures based on the overtone series. Since approximately 1600, Western music has overwhelmingly relied on three particular pitch collections: what we call *major*, *minor*, and the *chromatic* collections. First, let's clarify our terminology by defining melody, harmony, and pitch collection.

Melody

The term *melody* describes any succession of sounds. Any succession of sounds. It's as broad and non-subjective a definition as we can imagine and, therefore, it's the most useful. Melody, then, is the horizontal, the linear aspect of music, as sounds, usually in the form of notes, but not always, follow one another across some span of time.

Harmony

The term *harmony* describes the sound and relationship between pitches heard simultaneously, as sounding at the same time. Harmony, then, describes the vertical aspect of music, the relationship between pitches occurring simultaneously.

Pitch Collection

Despite its overwhelmingly common usage, the word scale is, from a conceptual point of view, used incorrectly a good 99% of the time. The word *scale* is derived from the Latin word for ladder. So, when we say "C-major scale," what is implied is a stepwise ordering of pitches, climbing up or climbing down. The word *scale*, therefore, cannot properly be used to address a group or set of pitches in which no ordering is implied. That's where the word *collection* comes in. By using the word, *collection*, no step-wise ordering is implied. Instead, the word *collection* addresses a group of pitches arrayed around a single, tonal center (or tonic) pitch. Thus, a *C-major collection* means a collection of pitches in the major mode, arrayed around the pitch C. Now, I know this might sound like terminological nit-picking, but by using the proper terminology, explanations, conceptualization, and comprehension will be much easier as we progress through our examination of pitch. Trust me on this, please.

Building a Pitch Collection 101

Most of us—unless we played in a way-too-loud rock band for way too long or stick our ipod earbuds halfway down our cochleae and then blast that sucker—most of us can hear sounds that range from a fundamental frequency of about 20 vibrations (or cycles) per second to about 20,000 cycles per second. It's a range of about 10 octaves (*octave* being a term we'll define in a moment). A large pipe organ can cover that entire 10-octave range; a modern piano covers a bit more than seven octaves. (For our information: Our 10-octave, 20 to 20,000 cycle range of hearing is not terribly impressive when compared to the animal kingdom as a whole. According to Douglas Giancoli, writing in his *Physics: Principles with Applications*, dogs can hear sounds as high as 50,000 cycles and bats can detect frequencies as high as 100,000 cycles.) However, even if we're not bats, we can still hear, for all intents and purposes, an infinite number of pitches. Just think of a siren moving through every possible pitch from 20 to 20,000 cycles and you'll understand what I mean. However, all the evidence would seem to indicate that we, as a species, are not equipped to deal musically with such an infinite range of pitch possibilities. So, any given musical culture must come up with a pitch collection, or a group of pitch collections, that serves its collective expressive and aesthetic needs. Different cultures have invented and employed different pitch collections, from the five-pitch collection traditionally used in Japanese music, to the 12-pitch collection currently used in Western music, to the 17-pitch collection used in some Arab musics, to the 43-pitch collection created by the 20th-century American composer, guru, crackpot, and prophet Harry Partch, to name just a few. What these and other pitch collections all have in common is the primacy of the interval called an *octave*.

Interval

An interval is the relationship between any two pitches. Again, an interval is the relationship between any two pitches.

The Interval of an Octave

The interval of an octave is, for music on this planet, the speed of light, the wall, the barrier past which we do not pass and which all terrestrial musical cultures have, thus far at least, acknowledged as the essential building block of their pitch systems. Aha! That's a statement to get everyone's attention! I'm going to play at the piano two pitches an octave apart. My question for all of us: Is the sound they create together a *consonance*? That is, do the pitches blend together, or is it a *dissonance*? That is, do they not seem to blend

©2007 The Teaching Company

together? [**Piano example:** octave Cs] Well, it's hard to tell I even played two different pitches, isn't it? I'll play them again: [**Piano example:** octave Cs] Whoa! Big time blend. Yes? In fact, those two pitches blend together so much that we don't really perceive them as being two different pitches at all; just the same pitch, one higher than the other, one lower than the other, as opposed to, for example, these two pitches. [**Piano example:** C and Db] No blend there! Those are two different pitches fer sure!

Back then, to this intervallic miracle that is the octave. The first Westerner to quantify just what an octave was, was the Greek mathematician, philosopher, and teacher Pythagoras. In 531 B.C.E. (that is, before the Common or Christian Era), Pythagoras emigrated from the Greek island of Samos to the southern Italian port city of what today is called Crotone, in Calabria, along the Gulf of Taranto. It was there, in Croton, as it was then known, that Pythagoras founded a school of philosophy and religion. The essential doctrine of his school was "a belief in the importance of numbers as a guide to the interpretation of the world." [The New Grove Dictionary of Music and Musicians, volume 15, 485] One of the things that had led Pythagoras to believe "in the importance of numbers as a guide to the interpretation of the world" was his discovery that basic numerical ratios corresponded to basic, blended musical intervals.

Here's what he did. Intent on determining what progressively complex numerical ratios actually sounded like, Pythagoras built something called a *monochord*, a fancy name for a single piece of string, a "mono–chord," tightly strung between two ends. For our demonstration purposes, our monochord will be this low pitch on the piano. [**Piano example:** low C] Pythagoras began at the beginning, by asking himself what a 1:1 ratio actually sounded like. He plucked the string [**Piano example:** low C] and then he plucked it again. [**Piano example:** low C] My friends, that's what a 1:1 ratio sounds like: it's…it's…why, it's exactly the same sound! It's a relationship called a *unison*, "uni–son," meaning "one sound."

The next step was to divide the string exactly in half and compare the sound produced by half the string to the original and, in doing so, hear what a 2:1 ratio sounds like. Well, here's what a 2:1 ratio sounds like. Here's the original string [**Piano example:** low C] and here's the pitch produced when we play half the string. [**Piano**

example: C one octave higher] When we play those two pitches together, they blend together seamlessly. [**Piano example:** C together with C one octave higher] What Pythagoras realized, and continued to realize, was that the simpler the numerical ratio between vibrating bodies, the more blended and therefore, the more consonant the sounds created by those vibrating bodies. This perception—the simpler and more basic the numerical ratio between vibrating bodies, the more consonant they sound—had profound meaning for Pythagoras and his fellow Greeks, who came to view music as the sonic manifestation of cosmic order. When we return, we'll pick back up with the octave and the sonic brick wall it represents in the creation of pitch systems. Thank you.

Lecture Eight
Pitch and Mode, Part 2

Scope:
The interval of an octave—the distance of eight white keys on the piano—is the most basic interval in our universe, a sonic manifestation of a 2:1 ratio. Different cultures divide the octave into various collections of pitches, which are then duplicated in higher or lower octaves. For thousands of years, Western culture divided the octave into seven different pitches. These pitch collections are called *diatonic* collections, or *modes*. The third degree of a diatonic collection imbues that collection with either a sense of brightness or a sense of darkness.

Outline

I. Pythagoras became aware of the paradox that pitches an octave apart represent: They blend together so profoundly that they do not sound like two different pitches so much as the same pitch. **Piano examples**: C below middle C and middle C.

   A. If each successive octave were divided into an entirely different set of pitches, cacophony would result. **Piano examples**.

   B. Virtually every musical culture on this planet has chosen to divide the octave into a single set of pitches that is then duplicated above and below in higher and lower octaves. **Piano examples**: Patty and Mildred Hill, *Happy Birthday* in octaves; C scale played an octave higher and an octave lower.

   C. When the word *octave* was coined, the Western pitch system consisted of seven different pitches (the white keys on the piano). The word *octave* represented the eight pitches from any one pitch to its duplicate, located eight pitches above or eight pitches below.

   D. The *chromatic collection* is a pitch collection that represents all the pitches on a modern keyboard.

      1. A chromatic collection divides the octave into 12 equal segments. **Piano example**: chromatic scale.

      2. The distance between the adjacent pitches is called a *semitone* or *half step*.

E. In Germanic-language cultures, alphabetical letters are used to identify the pitches. In Romance-language cultures, the pitches are identified by *solfège* syllables. **Piano example**: C-major scale denoted as do-re-me-fa-so-la-ti-do.

F. On the keyboard, the black keys lying between the white ones are collectively known and notated as *accidentals*: either sharps (symbol: #) or flats (symbol: b), depending on the key.

    1. The black key immediately to the upper right of any white key is called the sharp of that white key. For example, the black key immediately above C is called C-sharp.

    2. The black key immediately below any white key is called the flat of that white key.

    3. There is some ambiguity here because a sharp and a flat are the same key on the piano. For example, C-sharp and D-flat are the same key and sound the same pitch when played.

    4. Such pitches are called *enharmonic tones*; they sound the same but will be spelled as one pitch or the other, depending on whether the key uses sharps or flats. (We will discuss key signatures in Lecture Ten.)

II. Very little Western music uses all 12 pitches of the chromatic collection all the time, and that music dates from about 1910.

A. For thousands of years, Western music was characterized by pitch collections consisting of seven different pitches.

    1. These seven-pitch collections include the major and minor collections and the so-called church modes.

    2. A seven-pitch collection is called a *diatonic* collection.

    3. The Greek word *diatonic* means "proceeding by whole tones."

B. The intervallic content of adjacent pitches in a diatonic collection consists of five whole tones (one whole tone = two semitones) and two semitones. **Piano example**: C-major scale as an example of a diatonic collection.

C. The first pitch of a particular diatonic collection is called the *tonic* pitch. For example, in C major, C is the tonic.

1. The chromatic collection divides the octave into 12 different pitches; each adjacent pitch is a semitone, or half step, apart.

2. The C-major collection comprises the white keys on a piano, from C to C (five whole tones and two semitones).

D. The term *mode* also refers to diatonic collections.

1. As we understand them today, there are seven different modes (seven different diatonic collections).

2. Each one starts and ends on one of the seven pitches that are played by the seven white keys on the piano.

E. The Ionian mode, better known as the major scale, encompasses the white keys on the piano from a C to a C.

1. The intervallic profile of the Ionian mode (major scale) is: whole tone–whole tone–semitone–whole tone–whole tone–whole tone–semitone.

2. Whole tones are symbolized with the letter *T* and semitones are symbolized with the letter *S*. Thus, the major scale can be symbolized as: T–T–S| T–T–T–S. **Piano example**: C-major scale.

F. Much of the repertoire of plainchant is set in Dorian mode.

1. It encompasses the white keys on the piano from a D to a D and has an intervallic profile of: whole tone–semitone–whole tone–whole tone–whole tone–semitone–whole tone (T–S–T | T–T–S–T). **Musical selection**: Thomas of Celano, *Dies irae* (*Day of Wrath*, c. 1125).

2. The dark, somber sound of Dorian mode is largely due to the minor third—the distance of three semitones—between the tonic and third degree of the collection.

G. The Phrygian mode encompasses the white keys on the piano from an E to an E.

1. It has an intervallic profile of: semitone–whole tone–whole tone–whole tone–semitone–whole tone–whole tone (S–T–T | T–S–T–T).

2. The Phrygian mode has a stereotypically Spanish sound, produced by the semitone between the tonic and the second scale-degree of the mode and the whole tone between the tonic and the seventh scale-degree of the ode. **Piano examples**.

H. The Lydian mode encompasses the white keys on the piano from an F to an F.

   1. The Lydian mode is a bright and brilliant collection with an intervallic profile of: whole tone–whole tone–whole tone– semitone–whole tone–whole tone–semitone (T–T–T | S–T–T–S).

   2. Its brightness is largely due to the major third (a distance of four semitones) between the tonic and the third degree of the collection. **Piano example**: Lydian mode.

   3. It is of limited use in music because of its raised or augmented fourth (a tritone) between its tonic and fourth degree.

I. The Mixolydian mode encompasses the white keys on the piano from a G to a G.

   1. This is another bright mode as a result of the major third between the tonic and third degree of the collection.

   2. Its intervallic profile is: whole tone–whole tone–semitone–whole tone–whole tone–semitone–whole tone (T–T–S | T–T–S–T). **Piano example**: Mixolydian mode.

J. The Aeolian mode encompasses the white keys on the piano from an A to an A. Like the Dorian mode, it is dark and somber in character, with a minor third between its tonic and third degree.

   1. Its intervallic profile is: whole tone–semitone–whole tone–whole tone–semitone–whole tone–whole tone (T–S–T | T–S–T–T).

   2. The Aeolian mode, along with the Ionian mode (the major collection), is the most familiar diatonic collection to modern listeners. We know it as the minor collection or minor mode. **Piano example**: Aeolian mode. **Musical selection**: Ludwig van Beethoven, Symphony no. 3 in Eb Major, op. 55 (1803), movement 2, opening.

K. The Locrian mode encompasses the white keys on the piano from a B to a B.

1. Its intervallic profile is: semitone–whole tone–whole tone–semitone–whole tone–whole tone–whole tone (S–T–T | S–T–T–T). **Piano example**: Locrian mode.
2. Because of the diminished fifth (tritone) that lies between the tonic and the fifth degree of the mode, the Locrian mode is more a theoretical construct than of genuine musical use. **Piano example**: Locrian mode.

III. The seven diatonic collections or modes together constitute the backbone of pitch material in Western music from the ancient world through the early to mid-20th century.

    A. We hear them all again, back-to-back. **Piano examples**: Ionian, Dorian, Phrygian, Lydian, Mixolydian, Aeolian, and Locrian modes.

    B. By the 1600s, the number of modes in common use had been reduced to two: Ionian and Aeolian, which came to be known, respectively, as major and minor.

    C. More than any other factor, it is the third scale-degree of each of these modes that determines its relative brightness or darkness.

        1. The third degree of an Ionian mode is four semitones above the tonic, or first pitch. **Piano example**: four semitones.

        2. The third degree of the Aeolian mode is located three semitones above the tonic pitch. **Piano example**: three semitones.

        3. Borrowing from Latin nomenclature, where *major* means "larger" and *minor* means "smaller," the thirds that are four semitones in width are called major thirds and the thirds that are three semitones in width are called minor thirds.

        4. If the third degree of the mode is a major third (four semitones), the mode will have a brighter color

        5. If the third degree of the mode is a minor third (three semitones), the mode will have a darker color.

Lecture Eight—Transcript
Pitch and Mode, Part 2

This is Lecture Eight. It is entitled "Pitch and Mode, Part 2."

Building a Pitch Collection, Revisited

When we left off in Lecture Seven, we were discussing the interval of an octave as the essential intervallic building block of pitch systems on this particular planet. The first Westerner to quantify just what an octave was and why it was so special was the Greek mathematician, philosopher, and teacher Pythagoras, who lived between about 582 B.C.E. and 507 B.C.E. What Pythagoras discovered was that the simpler the numerical ratio between vibrating bodies, the more blended and, therefore, the more consonant the sounds created by those vibrating bodies. This perception, the simpler the numerical ratio between vibrating bodies, the more consonant the sound, had profound meaning for Pythagoras and his fellow Greeks, who came to view music as the sonic manifestation of cosmic order.

Pythagoras discovered that the simplest of all non-replicating numerical ratios, a 2:1 ratio, created the simplest of all intervallic relationships, one that we today call an octave. Pythagoras took a string and plucked it. [**Piano example:** C below middle C] He then divided that original string in half and plucked half the string. [**Piano example:** middle C] In doing so, he created a sound relationship, an interval, that is, the sonic manifestation of a 2:1 ratio. [**Piano example:** octave] In creating this interval, Pythagoras became aware of the amazing paradox represented by pitches an that describe a 2:1 ratio: they blend together so profoundly that they don't sound like two different pitches, but, rather, they sound like higher and lower versions of the same pitch.

The Brick Wall

Before we began discussing Pythagoras in Lecture Seven, we observed that while different cultures have invented all sorts of pitch collections, what these various pitch collections all have in common is the primacy of the octave. It all has to do with something called octave duplication. My friends, when creating a pitch collection, any given culture's got two choices. Choice number one is to divide each successive octave up and down into an entirely different set of pitches. I'll play you something like that on the piano, a long upwards scale in which the pitch collection changes from octave to octave. [**Piano example**] Now, cool as that might sound when played as a scale, let's consider what would happen if, for example, a man and a woman attempted to sing *Happy Birthday*, using a pitch collection like that one. Unless the woman is a former East German shot-putter, and unless the man is wearing leather slacks that, having gotten wet, have dried in the sun, they will be singing an octave apart, the woman an octave higher than the man. This, then, is what their performance is going to sound like, if they use different pitch collections in each octave. [**Piano example**: Patty and Mildred Hill, *Happy Birthday*] On those same lines, imagine what it would sound like if an orchestra, or chorus, were playing, or singing in such a way that adjacent octaves each utilized an entirely different set of pitches? Even for a modernist like myself, it would sound utterly random at best, awful at worst!

We were talking about the brick wall, the octave, and the two choices any given culture's got when creating a pitch collection. Choice one is to divide each successive octave into an entirely different set of pitches. Choice two is to divide a given octave into a single set of pitches that is then duplicated above and below, in higher and lower octaves. Thus, anything being sung or played in one octave will be sung or played on the same pitches in any other octave. Using such a system of octave duplication, our duet performance of *Happy Birthday* would sound like this. [**Piano example:** Patty and Mildred Hill, *Happy Birthday* in octaves] The same pitches just an octave apart. A most different story don't we think? The pitch collection on which *Happy Birthday* is based sees the octave divided into seven different pitches [**Piano example:** Professor Greenberg plays and counts the pitches of the scale of C] and then the duplicate, the octave above the first pitch, back to one and those same pitches are duplicated in every other octave, above [**Piano example:** scale of C above] and below. [**Piano example:** scale of C below]

As it turns out, virtually every musical culture on the planet has chosen this course: to divide the octave into some collection of pitches and to then duplicate those pitches in higher and lower octaves. At the time the word *octave* was coined, the Western pitch system consisted of seven different pitches, what we might think of as the white keys on the piano. In this seven-pitch system, the word *octave* represents the eight pitches from any one pitch to its duplicate, located eight pitches above, or eight pitches below.

The Chromatic Collection

We're going to require a visual tool for talking about pitch collections, a visual tool with which I trust we're all at least passingly familiar and that is a piano keyboard. An image of a keyboard with pitch names attached can be found in your lecture booklets. The chromatic collection, that pitch collection that represents all the pitches on a modern keyboard, is a product of thousands of years of musical evolution and we'll address the chromatic collection in greater detail, when we discuss its evolution in just a couple of lectures. For now, let's just make some observations. Observation one: the word *chromatic* comes from the Greek *chrōmatikos*, meaning "color" or "coloration." Let's think of the chromatic collection as the complete palette of pitches available in Western music. Observation two: The chromatic collection divides the octave into 12 equal segments. I would count those segments as I play a chromatic scale [**Piano example**] and back to where we started. Observation three: The distance between the adjacent pitches of the chromatic collection is called a *semitone* or a *half step*. So, adjacent pitches in the chromatic collection are called *semitones* or *half steps*.

Pitch Names

Looking at a keyboard, we are immediately struck by the arrangement of white keys and black keys, by which groups of two black keys alternate with groups of three black keys. The pitch C, which we are going to use as our starting point in this investigation, is the white key located immediately below (meaning to the left) of any group of two black keys. There are seven different white keys on the piano. I would play them and name them as we go. [**Piano example:** C-major scale]

Sidebar—Two Questions!

Why are the pitches named for letters, and why do we always seem to start these discussions on the pitch called C rather than on the pitch named after the first letter of the alphabet, the A? Good questions, my friends. Good questions. All right, question one: German and Germanic-language speaking cultures generally use letters to identify the pitches because it's clear, clean, and easy to remember! In Romance language-speaking cultures, the pitches are identified by what are called solfège syllables. [**Piano example:** Professor Greenberg plays a C-major scale and recites the solfège] Do-Re-Mi-Fa-So-La-Ti and then back to Do. Question two: Why, in discussions just like this one, do we typically start on the pitch C and not with the pitch A? And on those same lines, if C is so important, why wasn't it called *A* in the first place? All right, to answer that question we must get slightly ahead of ourselves, but that's okay. Historically, the pitch we call *A* was the more important pitch, as the white keys on a piano from an A to an A constitute a minor collection and when played as a scale, a minor scale [**Piano example:** A-minor scale], that scale, that minor mode, or minor collection, is a much older construct than the major mode, or major collection. The reason why we generally use a major collection as a starting point in an exploration such as this is a reflection of the growing importance of major over the last 400 years and the reason why we use C major is because it consists entirely of white keys on the piano and is, therefore, easier to visualize than any other major collection. We will, I promise, talk lots more about the nature and history of both the major and minor collections before the end of this lecture. But, for now: side bar over; back please, to pitch names.

The black keys on the keyboard are collectively known and notated as *accidentals*: either *sharps* [symbol: #], or *flats* [symbol: b], depending upon what key we are in. The black key immediately above (that is, to the upper right) of any white key is called a *sharp* of that white key. Therefore, the black key immediately above, or to the right of, a C is called a *C-sharp* (C#); the black key immediately above, or to the right of, an A would be called an *A-sharp* (A#). Conversely, the black key immediately below (that is, to the left) of any white key is called a *flat* of that white key. Therefore, the black key immediately below a D is called a *D-flat* (Db); the black key immediately below a B is called a *B-flat* (Bb) and so forth. Obviously, there's some ambiguity here, because a C# and a Db are the same key on the piano and sound as the same pitch when played. We say that C# and Db are enharmonic tones: They sound the same, but will be spelled as one pitch or the other depending upon whether we're in a key that uses flats or a key that uses sharps (all of which I'll explain when we get to key signatures in Lecture Ten).

Back to the chromatic collection. Very little Western music uses all 12 pitches of the chromatic collection all the time and the music that does dates from about 1910. For literally thousands of years, Western music was characterized, rather, by pitch collections consisting of seven different pitches. It is these seven-pitch collections, which include among them the major and minor collections as well as the so-called church modes, that now demand our attention.

Diatonic Collections

These seven-pitch collections are called *diatonic collections*. The word *diatonic* is Greek and it means "proceeding by whole tones." The diatonic collections that the ancient Greeks studied and codified came into existence long before the Greeks began to study them. As usual with music, theory and codification pretty much always follow practice. So, these are ancient, ancient modes. Here's our diatonic game plan: We will first define exactly what constitutes a diatonic collection. We'll then explore the intervallic content of diatonic collections, identify the different types of diatonic collections, or modes, as they are often called, and finish up this lecture by examining the two most important diatonic collections, major and minor. (My friends, a caveat as we begin: I'm going to play all our musical examples on a modern piano, using a tuning system that's only been standard since the 1850s. Obviously, we're not going to be hearing the nuances of pitch that the ancient Greeks, or medieval theorists, or the musicians of the Renaissance, Baroque, or Classical Eras, would have heard. That's okay; we work with the tools we have, meaning a modern piano. Besides, my lyre is in the shop.)

Diatonic Collection Defined

A diatonic collection is one that divides the octave into seven different pitches. The intervallic content of adjacent pitches in a diatonic collection will consist, by definition, of five whole tones and two semitones. Now, as an example of a diatonic collection, we return to our faithful and trusty C-major collection, that is, the white keys on a piano contained within octave Cs. Played as a scale, it sounds like this. [**Piano example:** C-major scale] Let's examine, please, as an example of a diatonic collection, the intervallic makeup of this particular collection, again, as an example of a diatonic collection in general and a major collection in particular. Please, we return to our image of a piano keyboard.

The Tonic Pitch

A new and very important word before we start. Since the pitch C is the parent pitch of this particular collection and since, therefore, the C will be the first pitch in a scalar presentation of this collection, we call the C the *tonic* pitch. Think of the word *tonic* as a contraction of the phrase *tonal center*, "tone center," "ton–ic." In C major, the pitch C is the tonic. As a reminder, we observed that the chromatic collection divides the octave into 12 different pitches and that adjacent pitches in a chromatic scale are a semitone (or half step) apart. [**Piano example:** chromatic scale] So, on to the intervallic makeup of a C-major collection (the white keys on a piano from C to C)!

We start on the tonic pitch, a C. Moving upwards, how many semitones is it from the C to the second pitch of the collection, a white key D? We count: From C upwards to a C# (that is, the black key directly above the C) is the distance of one semitone and from that black key C# upwards to the white key D is another semitone. So, the pitch D lies two semitones, or one whole tone, above the pitch C. A reminder: We are examining the intervallic makeup of a C-major collection, as an example of a diatonic collection in general and a major collection in particular. Okay, what is the distance from the second pitch of a C-major collection, a D, to the third pitch, an E? Using the keyboard as our visual guide, we count: From D up to the black key D# directly above it is one semitone and from that black key D# to the white key E directly above it is another semitone. So, from D to E, from the second to third pitches, or scale-degrees, of a C-major collection, is two semitones, or another whole tone.

Okay, we continue. What's the distance from the E, the third pitch, or third scale-degree, of a C-major collection to an F, the fourth pitch, or fourth scale-degree, of a C-major collection? E up to F—it is, my friends, a semitone, as there is no black key between an E and an F on a piano keyboard. Now, look, this drives a lot of people nuts. Yo! If it's a whole tone from a white key C to a white key D, and a whole tone from a white key D to a white key E, then why isn't it a whole tone from a white key E to a white key F? Because it isn't a whole tone. It isn't a whole step. It's a semitone. We cannot let our eyes lead our ears; just because both an E and an F are white keys on a piano doesn't mean that they are a whole tone apart. The interval, the sonic distance, between an E and an F is the same sonic distance as that between a C and a C#, or an A and an A#, or a D and a D#. It's a semitone. E and F are adjacent pitches in the chromatic collection and they sound a semitone apart. Period.

We continue our examination of the intervallic makeup of a C-major collection, as an example of a diatonic collection in general and a major collection in particular. From the F (the fourth scale-degree of a C-major collection) to a G (the fifth scale-degree of a C- major collection) is two semitones, or a whole step. From the G to the A (the sixth scale-degree of a C-major collection) is, again, two semitones or a whole step. From the A to the B (B being the seventh scale-degree of a C-major collection) is, again, two semitones, or a whole step. Finally, from B up to C is a semitone. There is no black key between a B and a C. So, it sounds like a semitone. Let's put it all together. The intervallic makeup of this C-major scale, that is, the distance from C to D, D to E, E to F, F to G, G to A, A to B and B back to C is: whole tone–whole tone–semitone (that semitone is from E to the F), whole tone–whole tone–whole tone–semitone (that final semitone is from the B up to the C). In the analytical and theoretical literature, in which a whole tone is abbreviated with the letter *T* (meaning "tone") and a semitone with the letter *S*, this means that adjacent pitches in a major collection describe an intervallic makeup of T–T–S | T–T–T–S. Now, we return to our definition of a diatonic collection: a seven-pitch division of the octave that will feature, by definition, five whole tones and two semitones. The major collection we just defined features five whole tones and two semitones.

The Diatonic Collections, or Modes

Mode is another word for *diatonic collection*. The word *collection*, as we've already discussed, is another and, I think, better word for a group of pitches that is all too frequently described as a scale. Now, please, we're not going to talk about the modes as they existed in either the ancient or medieval world. Such a discussion is as arcane, complex and, in regards to ancient practice, as speculative a musical discussion as any that exists and it goes far beyond what we're trying to achieve here in a listener's guide to music theory. Instead, we will discuss the modes (the various diatonic collections) as they are understood today. As we understand them today, there are seven different modes, seven different diatonic collections, each one starting and ending on one of the seven pitches represented by the seven white keys on the piano. Originally, these modes came into existence when the octave was divided into just seven different pitches, more or less the seven white keys on the piano. So, once again, we'll use the seven white keys of the piano as a visual aid in learning the seven modes. We start with:

The Ionian Mode

My friends, we've already discussed the Ionian mode in great detail. Better known as a major collection, the Ionian mode encompasses the white keys on the piano from C to C and has an intervallic profile of: T–T–S | T–T–T–S: whole tone–whole tone–semitone | whole tone–whole tone–whole tone–semi-tone. [**Piano example:** C-major scale] Under the heading of "we'll talk lots more about this in due time," we would nevertheless point out that the Ionian mode is a bright and brilliant sounding collection, something largely due to the major third (the distance of four semitones) between the tonic and third degree of the collection. Again, we'll get back to this before the end of the lecture. But, let's go on. We need to identify all seven of these diatonic modes. The second of these modes is:

The Dorian Mode

The Dorian mode is an ancient and hallowed pitch collection, as much of the repertoire of plainchant, or so-called Gregorian chant, is set in Dorian mode. Darker and more austere than the Ionian mode (for reasons we'll discuss in a few minutes), Dorian mode encompasses the white keys on the piano from D to D and has an intervallic profile of T–S–T | T–T–S–T. As a scale, the Dorian mode sounds like this. [**Piano example**] Let's hear the somber, serious sound of Dorian mode in action, in this singing of Thomas of Celano's plainchant trope *Dies irae* (*Day of Wrath*) of circa 1225. [**Musical selection:** Thomas of Celano, *Dies irae* (c. 1225)] The dark, somber sound of Dorian mode is largely due to the minor third, the distance of three semitones between the tonic and third degree of the collection.

Mode no. 3—The Phrygian Mode

The Phrygian mode encompasses the white keys of the piano from E to E and has an intervallic profile of S–T–T | T–S–T–T. That intervallic profile might not mean a whole heck-of-a-lot when I simply say it, but it's going to sound very familiar when I play it. [**Piano example:** E–D–E | E–F–G–A–G–F | E–D–E] There's a stereotypically Spanish sound, a distinctly Andalusian sound, to Phrygian mode. It's the semitone between the tonic and the second scale-degree of the mode and the whole tone between the tonic and seventh scale-degree of the mode that give the Phrygian mode its characteristically "Spanish" feel. [**Piano example:** melody in Phyrgian mode] Ole! Andalusia, my friends, is the southern-most region of Spain; its capital is Seville. The name *Andalusia* is derived from the Arabic *Al Andalulus*, which refers specifically to that part of the Iberian peninsula that was ruled by Muslims for 800 years, until 1492. The North African Moorish occupation profoundly influenced Andalusian culture and nowhere is that influence more apparent than in Andalusian flamenco song and dance, music that combines Andalusia's Greek, Phoenician, and Iberian heritage with that of North Africa and Arabia. The characteristic modal sound of this head-spinningly diverse music is that of the Phrygian mode.

Lydian Mode

Lydian mode encompasses the white keys on the piano from F to F. The Lydian mode is a bright and brilliant collection with an intervallic profile of T–T–T | S–T–T–S. The brightness and brilliance of the Lydian mode is largely due to the major third, the distance of four semitones between the tonic and third degree of the collection. Let's hear a little Lydian mode, please. [**Piano example**] Again, under the heading of TMI ("too much information"), I would tell you that the Lydian mode is of limited musical use in tonal music because of something called a raised, or augmented, fourth. The fourth scale-degree of Lydian mode is what we call an *augmented* fourth, or a *tritone*, above the tonic, rather than an interval called a *perfect* fourth. Let's focus, for a moment, on this augmented fourth. [**Piano example**] This augmented fourth between the tonic and fourth degrees of the mode imbue the Lydian mode with a peculiar sort of sound and generally puts it outside the pale of harmonic usage, as harmonic usage developed in the 15th and 16th centuries.

Look, I told you that that was too much information, but, assuming you listen to this course more than once, it will make lots of sense in light of what we will discuss in later lectures! Meanwhile, we move on to the fifth of our modes.

To the Mixolydian Mode!

Mixolydian mode encompasses the white keys on the piano from a G to a G. Like the Ionian mode and Lydian mode, the Mixolydian mode is a bright mode as a result of the major third (the distance of four semitones) between the tonic and third degrees of the collection. Overall, the Mixolydian mode has an intervallic profile of T–T–S | T–T–S–T. [**Piano example**] The sixth of our modes is:

The Aeolian Mode

Aeolian Mode encompasses the white keys on a piano from an A to an A. Like Dorian mode, it is dark and somber in character with a minor third between its tonic and third degree; its intervallic profile is T–S–T | T–S–T–T. Along with the Ionian mode, which, as we observed, is better known as the major collection, the Aeolian mode is the most familiar diatonic collection to modern listeners. My friends, we know it as the minor collection, or as the minor mode. [**Piano example**] With certain important modifications, which we'll talk about in Lecture Fifteen, the minor collection, or minor mode, has been ubiquitous in Western music for the last 400 plus years. As an example of its darkness and sobriety, let's hear the opening of the second movement funeral march from Beethoven's Symphony no. 3 of 1803. [**Musical selection:** Beethoven, Symphony no, 3 in Eb Major, op. 55 (1803), movement 2, opening]

Locrian Mode

The seventh and last of our modes is the Locrian mode. The Locrian mode encompasses the white keys on the piano from a B to a B and is dark and quite dissonant in tone, with an intervallic profile of S–T–T | S–T–T–T. It sounds like this. [**Piano example**] More TMI, my friends; more "too much information." The Locrian mode is almost never used because of the diminished fifth (or tritone) that lies between the tonic and fifth scale-degree of the mode. As we will learn in Lecture Nine, the second most important pitch in any diatonic collection, after the first, or tonic pitch, is the one that lies an interval of a perfect fifth above that tonic. Well, the fifth degree of a Locrian mode does not lie a perfect fifth above the tonic, but rather, a diminished fifth. It's a semitone smaller than a perfect fifth. Let me demonstrate that. Here's what a perfect fifth would sound like above the tonic of a Locrian mode. [**Piano example**] But, of course, a Locrian mode does not have that perfect fifth. It has a diminished fifth that sounds like this. [**Piano example**] Yeah, from a tonal harmonic standpoint, this diminished fifth renders the Locrian mode almost useless. Like the silent *gh* in words like *fight, blight, might*, and *Haight* (as in "Ashbury"), we know that the Locrian mode is there, but, excepting some applications in jazz, very little, if any, music is actually set in Locrian mode. Again, this will make much more sense in light of information to come in future lectures. This I promise.

One last thing before we start putting all this modal stuff together. The names by which we presently identify the diatonic modes—Ionian, Dorian, Phrygian, and so forth—were coined in the ancient world, but were misapplied and misinterpreted during the early Middle Ages. It was a case of mistaken identity, unwittingly perpetrated by the music theorists and practitioners of the early church. You see, these good people read and studied what ancient texts said about music, ancient texts that became the basis of their own research and theorizing. Unfortunately, the problem was that these early medieval theorists had not a single decipherable note of ancient music available to them, so when it came to actually applying the ancient texts to the modes as they understood them, they were truly in the dark, operating on a wing and a prayer. Aristotle, writing in his book *Politics*, noted that and we quote Aristotle: "The musical modes differ essentially from one another, and those who hear them are differently affected by each. Some of them make men sad and grave, like the so-called 'Mixolydian'; others enfeeble the mind; another, again, produces a moderate and settled temper, which appears to be the peculiar effect of the Dorian; [and] the Phrygian inspires enthusiasm." [Grout/Palisca, 4th edition, 16] Look, today, we would never consider the relatively bright Mixolydian mode, with its major third between the tonic and third scale-degree, as being "sad and grave" and, the cultural differences between ourselves and the ancient Greeks notwithstanding, neither would they. The medieval theorists misapplied the names and it's a case of mistaken identity that has stuck. All right.

Putting Mode All Together

The seven diatonic collections or modes constitute the very backbone of pitch material in Western music from the ancient world through the early to mid-20th century. Let's hear them again, back-to-back: the Ionian mode [**Piano example**]; the Dorian mode [**Piano example**]; the Phrygian mode [**Piano example**]; the Lydian mode [**Piano example**]; the Mixolydian mode [**Piano example**]; the Aeolian mode [**Piano example**] and the Locrian mode [**Piano example**]. By the 1600s, the number of modes in common use had been reduced to two: the Ionian mode and the Aeolian mode, what came to be known as, respectively, major and minor.

Major and Minor Properly Defined

The words *major* and *minor* often cause some confusion in their application to music. It's not the words themselves, but, rather, our contemporary usage that has rendered the meaning of *major* and *minor* confusing. Look, today, the words *major* and *minor* have taken on subjective meanings: The word *major* is used to describe something we deem as being of overriding importance; while the word *minor* usually describes something of lesser import. This subjective usage has nothing to do with what major and minor mean as musical terms. As musical terms, *major* and *minor* come from Middle English words based on the Latin *maior* and *minor*, meaning, respectively, "larger" and "smaller," for example, as in the constellations *Ursa major* and *Ursa minor* ("Big Bear" and "Little Bear").

Let's illustrate the musical usage of *major* and *minor* using the seven diatonic modes and in doing so, clarify our earlier observations regarding the relative brightness or darkness of the modes. As we observed previously, Ionian mode (or the major mode), Lydian mode, and Mixolydian mode are relatively bright in character and Dorian mode, Phrygian mode, Aeolian mode (or the minor mode), and Locrian mode are relatively dark in character. Let me explain why and, in doing so, anticipate the exploration of intervals that will dominate our next lecture. More than any other factor, my friends, it is the third scale-degree of each of these modes that determines its relative brightness or darkness.

Let's start with the Ionian mode, or the major collection, the white keys on the piano from C to C. Let's count how many semitones distant the third degree of the collection (the pitch E) is from the tonic (the pitch C). Counting upwards, from C to C#, is one semitone. [**Piano example**] From C# to D is two semitones. [**Piano example**] From D to D# is three semitones [**Piano example**] and, finally, from D# to E is four semitones. [**Piano example**] So, the third degree of an Ionian mode is four semitones above the tonic, or first pitch and I would tell you that the same thing is true of a Lydian mode and a Mixolydian mode: The third degree of each of those brighter sounding modes is also located four semitones above the tonic, or first pitch.

Let's do the same thing, now, with an Aeolian, or minor mode, the white notes on the piano from an A to an A. Counting upwards, from A to A#, is one semi-tone. [**Piano example**] From A# to B is two semitones [**Piano example**] and from B to C, C being the third degree of an Aeolian mode starting on A, is three semitones [**Piano example**] and I would tell you the same thing is true of a Dorian mode, a Phrygian mode and a Locrian mode: The third degree of each of these modes is also located three semitones above the tonic pitch.

Because it spans three upwards scale-steps, the distance from the tonic to the third pitch of each mode is called the interval (the distance) of a third. Some of the thirds we've just examined (the ones from the brighter modes) are, at four semitones in width, bigger (wider) than the ones from the darker modes, which are three semitones in width. Borrowing from Latin nomenclature, where *major* means "larger" and *minor* means "smaller," the thirds that are four semitones in width are called major thirds and the thirds that are three semitones in width are called minor thirds. The third degree of any diatonic collection, or mode, is called the *color tone* and now we can see why. If that third degree, or color tone, is a major third above the tonic, the mode will have a brighter color; if it is a minor third above the tonic, the mode will have a darker color.

Conclusions and Review

We will talk lots more about major and minor collections and intervals when we return, but first, my friends, a quick review of what we've covered in these last two lectures. What we perceive as sound is the result of a concussion wave: tiny fluctuations in air pressure. Our hearing apparatus, though admittedly inferior when compared to some animals, is nevertheless wonderfully sensitive and our ability to sort out and comprehend incredibly complex combinations of sounds is nothing short of amazing! A noise sound is one in which there is so much acoustical information present that it is impossible for us to perceive any particular fundamental pitch. A discrete sound is a sound that features a single, perceivable, fundamental frequency; a discrete sound is one that we can sing. A pitch is a discrete sound with the attribute of timbre. A note is a pitch that has a specific duration. The acoustic distance between any two pitches is called an interval. The interval of an octave (the distance of eight ["oct-ave"] white keys on the piano) is the most basic interval in our universe, a sonic manifestation of a 2:1 ratio. Different cultures divide the octave up into various collections of pitches, which are then duplicated in higher and lower octaves. For literally thousands of years, Western culture divided the octave into seven different pitches, into pitch collections called diatonic collections, or diatonic modes. By around the year 1600, two of these seven diatonic modes had become pre-eminent: the Ionian mode, which became known as the major mode, or major collection, and the Aeolian mode, which became known as the minor mode, or minor collection. More than any other single pitch, it is the third degree of a diatonic collection, the so-called color tone that imbues the collection with either a sense of brightness, or darkness. In the major mode, that third degree is four semitones, or a major third, above the tonic. In the minor mode, that third degree is three semitones, or a minor third, above the tonic. Lot's of information, much of it very complex, but we will keep working and keeping explaining as we move forward. Thank you.

Semitone Chart

Minor Second:	1 semitone
Major Second:	2 semitones
Minor Third:	3 semitones
Major Third:	4 semitones
Perfect Fourth:	5 semitones
Augmented Fourth (Tritone):	6 semitones
Diminished Fifth (Tritone):	6 semitones
Perfect Fifth:	7 semitones
Minor Sixth:	8 semitones
Major Sixth:	9 semitones
Minor Seventh:	10 semitones
Major Seventh:	11 semitones
Octave:	12 semitones

Keyboard

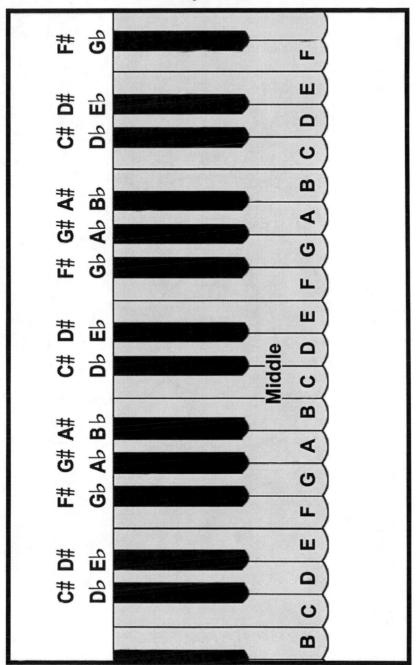

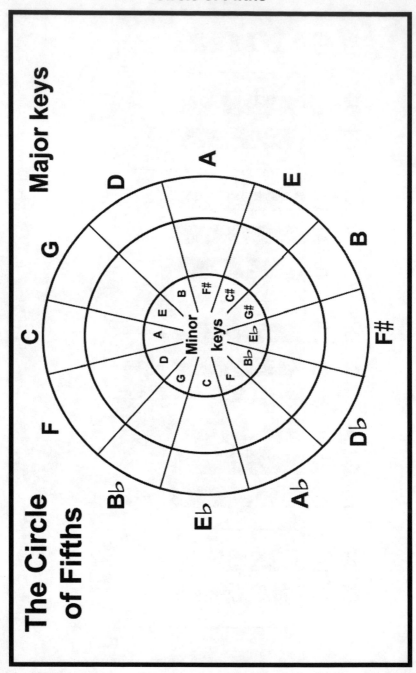

The Circle
of Fifths

Major keys

Minor keys

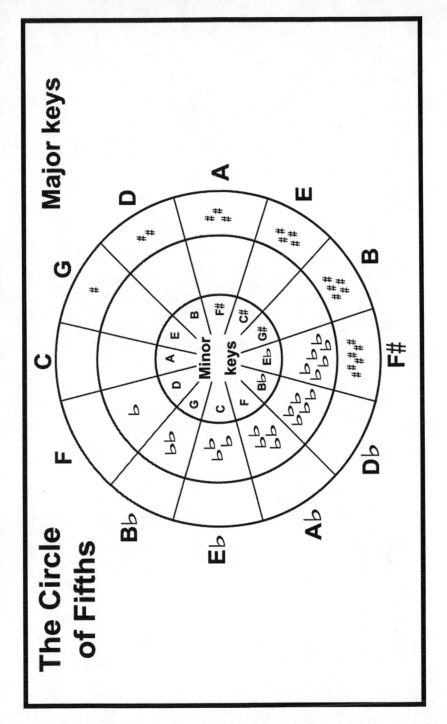

The Circle of Fifths

Major keys

Minor keys

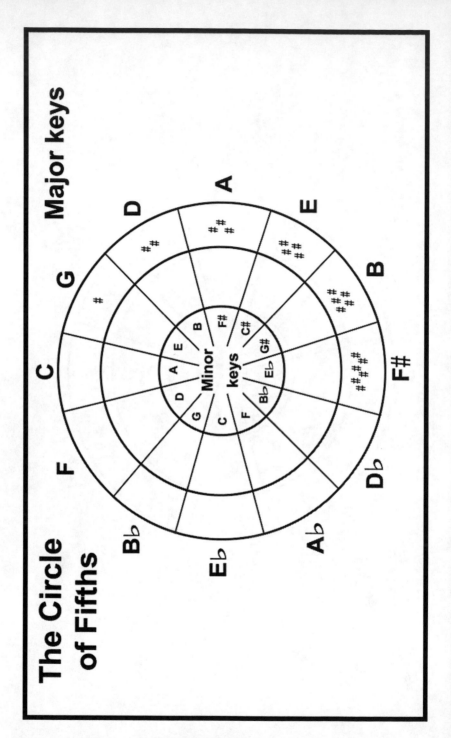

The Circle of Fifths

Major keys

Minor keys

©2007 The Teaching Company

Timeline

500 B.C.E. .... Pythagoras postulates his theory that music is a microcosm of the cosmos and ruled by the same mathematical laws that operate in all of the universe.

320 B.C.E. .... Aristoxenus writes his book on harmonic elements.

1100s–1300s .... Emergence of three- and four-voice harmonic textures and development of triadic harmony in a polyphonic texture.

1400s–1500s .... Emergence of mean-tone tuning and composed homophony.

1596 .... Tsai-Yu of China describes the principle of equal temperament, though traditionally, Andreas Werckmeister is credited with inventing this concept in 1700.

1500s–1900 .... Development and cultivation of functional tonality.

1600 .... Jacopo Peri's *Euridice*, the first complete opera to survive to modern times, heralded the rise of opera. This led to the development of instrumental genres, which in turn, influenced functional harmony.

1600s–1750s .... The Baroque Era; Johann Sebastian Bach uses well-tempered tuning, the forerunner of equal-tempered tuning; word melody gradually yields to vocal melody, vocally conceived instrumental melody, and instrumental melody.

1600–1900 .... Common Practice Period.

1700 ....According to conventional Western history, Andreas Werckmeister invents the concept of equal temperament.

1730s–1820s ....The Classical Era; Beethoven makes unprecedented use of meter and syncopation as the principal thematic material and dominant feature of musical texture.

1820s–1890s ....The Romantic Era; the limits of functional tonality are increasingly stretched; Hector Berlioz takes the exploration of orchestral timbre to new heights.

1850s...Equal temperament becomes standard.

1859 ....The French recommend the standard or concert pitch of A = 435, by which orchestras should be tuned; Richard Wagner's *Tristan und Isolde*.

1885 ....International conference in Vienna recommends adoption of the French standard pitch of A = 435.

1900 ....Functional harmony begins to yield to freer concepts of tonality; experimental meters, including asymmetrical meter, additive meter, and syncopation begin to be used on an unprecedented scale.

1910 ....Claude Debussy's preludes for piano exemplify his use of the whole-tone collection.

1912 ....Igor Stravinsky's *The Rite of Spring* cultivates asymmetrical meter to a degree entirely new in European music; Arnold Schönberg's *Pierrot Lunaire* employs non-lyrical vocal technique and freely atonal music.

1939 ....International conference adopts the standard or concert pitch of A = 440.

Glossary

Accidental: A notational sign/symbol that modifies a pitch. See also **Sharp**, **Flat**, and **Natural**.

Additive meter: Some combination of beats grouped in twos and threes.

Aria: Originally a song sung by a single voice with or without accompaniment, now taken to mean a lyric song for solo voice usually expressing intense emotion.

Asymmetrical meter: Exhibits no particular repeated metric pattern.

Atonal/atonality: Music lacking the sense of a central pitch, as opposed to tonal/tonality.

Augmented: Major or perfect interval extended by a semitone; e.g., augmented sixth: C–A-sharp.

Bar: See **Measure**.

Bar lines: Notational device: two vertical lines that enclose a measure; one metric unit.

Beat: Smallest pulse to which we can comfortably move our bodies. See also **Meter**.

Cadence: Harmonic or melodic formula that occurs at the end of a phrase, section, or composition, conveying a momentary or permanent conclusion; in other words, a musical punctuation mark.

Cadenza: Passage for solo instrument in an orchestral work, usually a concerto, designed to showcase the player's skills.

Canon: Strict counterpoint in which each voice exactly imitates the previous voice at a fixed distance.

Chord: Simultaneous sounding of three or more different pitches.

Chromatic: Scale in which all the pitches are present. On a keyboard, this translates as moving consecutively from white keys to black keys.

Classical: Designation given to works of art of the 17th and 18th centuries, characterized by clear lines and balanced form.

Closed cadence: Equivalent to a period or an exclamation mark; such a cadence ends on the tonic and gives a sense of rest and resolution.

Compound meter: Any meter that features a triple subdivision within each beat.

Concert A: Pitch to which Western orchestral players tune their instruments before a performance: A = 440.

Conjunct: Melodic contour that generally features steps between pitches; such a melody will usually sound smooth and controlled.

Counterpoint/contrapuntal textures: From the Latin *punctus contra punctum*, or "note against note"; a style of writing that emphasizes the rhythmic independence of the voices. See also **Polyphony**.

Deceptive/false cadence: Equivalent to a colon or semicolon; such a cadence brings resolution but not to the expected tonic harmony.

Diatonic: Greek word meaning "proceeding by whole tones"; a seven-pitch collection.

Diminished: Minor or perfect interval that is reduced by one semitone, e.g.: minor seventh, C–B-flat, becomes diminished when the minor is reduced by one semitone to become C-sharp–B-flat. Diminished sevenths are extremely unstable harmonies that can lead in a variety of harmonic directions.

Disjunct: Melodic contour that generally features leaps between pitches; such a melody will usually sound jagged and jumpy.

Dominant: Pitch and chord five pitches above a given tonic pitch/chord. The dominant harmony is the chord most closely related to the tonic chord in a given key; the dominant chord will almost always immediately precede an appearance of the tonic chord.

Duple meter: Metrical pattern featuring accented beats every two or four beats.

Dynamics: Degrees of loudness, e.g., *piano* (quiet), *forte* (loud), indicated in a musical score.

Enharmonic: Pitches that are identical in sound but with different spellings, depending on the key context, e.g., C-sharp and D-flat.

Equal tempered: see **Temperament**.

Fermata: Pause.

Flat: Accidental (sign/symbol) placed to the left of a note indicating that the pitch should be lowered by a semitone.

Frequency: Rate of vibration of a string, column of air, or other sound-producing body.

Functional harmony: Harmonic usage that was standardized and codified into a fully coherent system during the Baroque period. This method is still used by modern arrangers and orchestrators. The basic concept used in functional harmony is the fact that all harmonic sounds used in music may be classified in three large groups. These groups derive their names from the three important roots of the traditional harmonic system: the tonic, dominant, and subdominant. In this way, they are comparable to the three primary colors used by the artist: red, yellow, and blue.

Fundamental frequency: Rate of vibration of the full length of a sound-producing body and the sound created by that full-length vibration.

Graded dynamics: Markings used to indicate a progressive increase in loudness or softness, respectively, *crescendo* ("getting louder") or *decrescendo/ diminuendo* ("getting softer/quieter").

Half step: See **Semitone**.

Hemiola: Temporary use of a displaced accent to produce a feeling of changed meter without actually changing the meter.

Home key: Main key of a movement or composition. See also **Key**.

Homophonic texture/homophony: Texture in which one melodic line predominates; all other melodic material is heard as being secondary or accompanimental.

Interval: Distance between two pitches, e.g.: C–G (upwards) = a fifth.

Inversion: Loosely applied to indicate a reversal in melodic direction. Harmonic inversion is a situation in which a chord tone other than the root is in the bass.

Just intonation: see **Temperament**.

K. numbers: Köchel numbers, named after Ludwig von Köchel, who catalogued Mozart's works.

Key: Collection of pitches that relate to a specific major or minor mode.

Klangfarbenmelodie: Term coined by composer Arnold Schönberg to describe a style of composition that employs several different kinds of tone colors to a single pitch or to multiple pitches. This is achieved by distributing the pitch or melody among several different instruments.

Major: Modern term for Ionian mode; characterized by an intervallic profile of whole tone–whole tone–semitone–whole tone–whole tone–whole tone–semitone (symbolized as: T–T–S| T–T–T–S).

Measure: Metric unit; space between two bar lines.

Melody: Any succession of pitches.

Meter: Group of beats organized in a regular rhythmic pattern and notated in music as a time signature.

Minor: Modern term for Aeolian mode; characterized by an intervallic profile of whole tone–semitone–whole tone–whole tone–semitone–whole tone–whole tone (symbolized as T–S–T | T–S–T–T).

Modal ambiguity: Harmonic ambiguity, in which the main key is not clearly identified.

Mode: Major or minor key (in modern Western usage).

Monophonic texture/monophony: Texture consisting of only a single, unaccompanied melody line.

Motive/motif: Brief succession of pitches from which a melody grows through the processes of repetition, sequence, and transformation.

Movement: Independent section within a larger work.

Natural: Accidental (sign/symbol) placed to the left of a note, indicating that the note should not be sharpened or flattened; a white key on a keyboard.

Note: Pitch that has been notated.

Octatonic scale: Scale of eight pitches per octave, arranged by alternating half steps and whole steps.

Open cadence: Equivalent to a comma; such a cadence pauses on the dominant harmony without resolving to the tonic harmony, creating tension and the need to continue.

Pedal note: Pitch sustained for a long period of time, against which other changing material is played. A pedal harmony is a sustained chord serving the same purpose.

Pentatonic scale: Scale of five tones. It is used in African, Far Eastern, and Native American music. The pentatonic scale has been used in 20th-century Western compositions, as well.

Pitch: Discrete sound with the attributes of timbre and duration.

Pivot modulation: Change of key achieved via a pitch or pitches common to two chords.

Pizzicato: Plucked pitches.

Plagal/amen cadence: Generally occurs as a musical postscript following a closed cadence.

Plainchant/Gregorian/Old Roman chant: One of the earliest surviving styles of music in western Europe, attributed to Pope Gregory the Great. In reality, Gregory probably had little to do with the chant we know today, because the chants that survive in manuscripts date from the 11th to the 13th centuries, and Gregory died in the year 604. The surviving chants are modal, with monophonic melodies and freely flowing, unmeasured vocal lines. Most chants belong to the Mass or to the daily offices.

Polyphonic texture/polyphony (contrapuntal texture or counterpoint): Texture consisting of two or more simultaneous melody lines of equal importance.

Pythagorean comma: Discrepancy between the opening pitch and the last pitch in a circle of fifths, making the final pitch about an eighth of a tone sharp.

Recitative: Operatic convention in which the lines are half sung, half spoken.

Ritardando: Gradually getting slower (abbreviation: ritard.).

Scale: All the pitches inside a given octave, arranged stepwise so that there is no duplication. The pitches of the Western scales were derived initially by Pythagoras and his division of a vibrating string into basic ratios. The names of the chords built on the scale-steps are: tonic, supertonic, mediant, sub-dominant, dominant, sub-mediant, leading tone.

Semitone: Smallest interval in Western music; on the keyboard, the distance between a black key and a white key, as well as B–C and E–F.

Sequence: Successive repetitions of a motive at different pitches; compositional technique for extending melodic ideas.

Sharp: Accidental (sign/symbol) placed to the left of a note, indicating that the pitch should be raised by a semitone.

Sprechstimme: Vocal style in which the melody is spoken at approximate pitches rather than sung on exact pitches. The *Sprechstimme* was developed by Arnold Schönberg.

Syncopation: Displacement of the expected accent from a strong beat to a weak beat and vice versa.

Temperament: System of tuning in which, by way of compensating for the Pythagorean comma, some of the intervals are altered slightly from their acoustically pure ratios in order to allow instruments to play in most or all keys without undue harshness. Examples: just intonation (Pythagorean), mean-tone tuning, well temperament, and equal temperament (modern Western usage).

Tempo: Relative speed of a passage of music.

Texture: Number of melodies present and the relationship between those melodies in a given segment of music; they include monophony, polyphony (counterpoint), heterophony, and homophony.

Theme: Primary musical subject matter in a given section of music.

Timbre: Tone color.

Tonal/Tonality: Sense that one pitch is central to a section of music, as opposed to atonal/atonality.

Tonic: Home pitch and chord of a piece of tonal music. Think of the term as being derived from "tonal center" (*tonic*). For example, if a movement is in C, the pitch C is the tonic pitch and the harmony built on C is the tonic chord.

Triad: Chord consisting of three pitches: root, third, and fifth, e.g.: C/E/G, triad of C major.

Triple meter: Metrical pattern having three beats to a measure.

Tune: Generally singable, memorable melody with a clear sense of beginning, middle, and end.

Well tempered: See **Temperament**.

Whole-tone collection: Divides the octave into six equal segments; a whole-tone scale ascends and descends by major seconds, or whole tones.

Biographical Notes

Aristoxenus (c. 364–304 B.C.E.): Greek philosopher and writer on music and rhythm; discovered harmonic elements in 320 B.C.E.

Milton Babbitt (b. 1916): American composer, teacher, theorist, and exponent par excellence of total serialism.

Johann Sebastian Bach (1685–1750): One of the greatest composers who ever lived, Bach's unsurpassed genius graced all genres of Baroque instrumental and vocal music except opera. His music combines intellectual rigor and structural control with exuberant and profuse melodic content. His influence on later generations of composers was profound.

Ludwig van Beethoven (1770–1827): German composer and pianist who radically transformed every musical form in which he worked; considered a key transitional figure between the Classical and Romantic Eras because of his Classical training and technique and Romantic range of expression. His music combined the spirit of the Enlightenment, the spirit of revolution, and the turmoil of the Napoleonic Era with his own personality.

Hector Berlioz (1803–1869): French composer who introduced the concept of an *idée fixe*, a single melody that unites an entire work but is gradually transformed throughout the course of the work. The first composer to closely associate his music with extra-musical programs.

Johannes Brahms (1833–1897): German composer whose compositions synthesize Classical forms with subtle, often highly impassioned expressive content and a propensity for intricate rhythms; considered a master of the German *lied*.

Dave Brubeck (b. 1920): One of the best known jazz pianists and composers, whose compositional output represents some of the finest 20th-century American jazz.

Frédéric Chopin (1810–1849): Polish-born composer who devoted himself almost exclusively to solo piano compositions that are masterpieces of subtlety and expressive nuance, unique in the repertoire. Chopin was the quintessentially Romantic composer, whose music was inspired by, and perfectly tailored to, the newly developed piano.

Claude Debussy (1862–1918): French composer who was the founder and most important representative of the Impressionist Movement in music, marking a significant break with the German musical tradition of his time.

George Frederick Handel (1685–1759): German composer of the Baroque Era whose works are characterized by grandeur and sustained power, simple melodies, and breadth and clarity of harmonic structures. Handel was responsible for the phenomenal popularity of the English-language oratorio.

Franz Joseph Haydn (1732–1809): Austrian composer who is regarded as the father of the symphony and string quartet because he defined and standardized the external and internal structures of those musical genres. His inventive genius, solid craftsmanship, and exuberant wit exerted a profound influence on younger composers, such as Mozart.

Scott Joplin (1868–1917): American composer and pianist whose ragtime music was revived in the movie *The Sting* (1974), bringing Joplin the justly deserved renown he never experienced in his own lifetime.

Ludwig von Köchel (1800–1877): In 1862, von Köchel published a chronological and thematic register of the works of Mozart. It is sometimes known today as the Köchel catalogue, and the so-called *K. numbers* are still used to refer to Mozart's works.

Gustav Mahler (1860–1911): Bohemian composer whose output consists almost entirely of late-Romantic-style symphonies and *lieder*. He used the Classical forms of sonata and scherzo to frame a highly expressive harmonic and melodic palette, reflecting the *fin-de-siécle* mood of anxiety that took hold of Europe during his era.

Wolfgang Mozart (1756–1791): One of the greatest of all Western composers, Mozart possessed an impeccable sense of form and symmetry that was allied to an infallible craftsmanship and graced with what many have considered a "divine" inspiration. His musical genius produced a prolific number of masterpieces in every genre, representing the Classical style at its zenith.

Modest Mussorgsky (1839–1881): One of the five composers in Balakirev's group inspired by Russian folk melodies and rhythms; his *Boris Godunov* is the pinnacle of Russian opera.

Carl Nielsen (1876–1939): Danish composer whose music took a highly original approach to late musical Romanticism.

"King" Oliver (1885–1938): American jazz cornetist, bandleader, and composer who represents the finest of the New Orleans jazz style. The recordings he made with Louis Armstrong were the most influential of any early jazz recordings.

Jacopo Peri (1561–1633): One of the members of the Florentine Camerata, whose ideas laid the foundations for the evolution of opera. Peri's opera *Euridice* (1600) is the first complete opera to survive to modern times.

Pythagoras (c. 560–480 B.C.E.): Greek philosopher who theorized that music is a microcosm of the cosmos and ruled by the same mathematical laws that operate throughout the universe.

Samuel Scheidt (1587–1654): German organist, composer, and teacher of the late Renaissance/early Baroque Era; a skilled polyphonist who combined polyphony with Italian concerto style.

Arnold Schönberg (1874–1951): Viennese-born composer who developed the concept of *emancipation of dissonance*, through which he attempted to "free" his music from the shackles of traditional tonality. *Pierrot Lunaire* (1912) was the capstone to Schönberg's freely atonal period.

Robert Schumann (1810–1856): German composer, pianist, conductor, and critic. Schumann was noted for his poetic works, which fuse Classical structure with Romantic expression. His songs, particularly his song-cycles, are among the glories of *lieder*.

John Philip Sousa (1854–1932): American bandmaster and composer, known for his brilliant marches, of which *The Stars and Stripes Forever* is the most famous.

Johann Strauss II (1825–1899): Known as the "Waltz King," Strauss was the most renowned member of a family of composers of popular music and light opera; his *Blue Danube Waltz* is one of the most famous pieces of music ever written.

Richard Strauss (1864–1949): German composer who shone in two major areas: tone poem and opera. Almost single-handedly, he carried the Wagnerian opera tradition and the Romantic Lisztian tone poem into the 20th century. He is also one of the great composers of *lieder*.

Igor Stravinsky (1882–1971): Russian-born composer whose works are marked by nationalism and revolutionary use of rhythm and melody. His *The Rite of Spring* (1912) is one of the most extraordinary musical compositions of the 20th century.

Peter Ilyich Tchaikovsky (1840–1893): Widely popularized Russian composer, whose music is characterized by extreme tunefulness and emotional fervor, typical of Romantic musical trends.

Georg Philipp Telemann (1681–1767): German composer who mastered the Baroque German and Italian compositional styles and whose compositions represent the best of Baroque music.

Thomas of Celano (c. 1200–1255 C.E.): Franciscan monk believed to have composed the Catholic plainchant prayer for the dead *Dies irae* around 1225.

Tsai-Yu: Ming dynasty prince who described the principle of equal temperament in 1596, though traditionally Andreas Werckmeister is credited with inventing this concept in 1700.

Giuseppe Verdi (1813–1901): Prolific Italian composer whose career practically constitutes the history of Italian opera between 1850 and 1900. Verdi's style evolved slowly and almost entirely eliminates the differentiation between aria and recitative, elevating the orchestra and favoring characterization and dramatic truth over the vocal prettiness of the bel canto style.

Antonio Vivaldi (1678–1741): Italian composer and violinist. His importance lies in his concertos, for their boldness and originality and for their central place in the history of concerto form.

Richard Wagner (1813–1883): German composer who brought German Romantic opera to its culmination. Some of his most influential musical innovations include *continuous music*, the *leitmotif*, the *Gesamtkunstwerke*, and the development of the orchestra into full partnership with the voices.

Bibliography

Baker, Theodore, and Nicholas Slonimsky. *Pocket Manual of Musical Terms*. New York: Schirmer, 1995. An absolutely indispensable little handbook (inexpensive, too) that contains definitions, pronunciations, elements of music notation, and a biographical list of famous musicians.

Giancoli, Douglas C. *Physics: Principles with Applications*. New York: Prentice-Hall, 2002. Contains a chapter on the characteristics of sound, including pitch and frequency.

Grout, Donald, and Claude Palisca. *A History of Western Music*, 4th ed. New York: W. W. Norton, 1988. The standard academic music history text, it can be purchased with an anthology of all the music discussed in the text as well as a CD set containing recordings of all the music in the anthology.

Schonberg, Harold. *The Lives of the Great Composers*, 3rd ed. New York: W. W. Norton, 1997. Excellent and entertaining vignette-style biographies of "the great composers."

Webster's Seventh New Collegiate Dictionary. Springfield, MA: G. and C. Merriam Company, 1963.

Notes